THE BOOK OF FAIRS

BRUGES HAD A GENIUS FOR PAGEANTRY

The Book of FAIRS

by HELEN AUGUR

*With an Introduction
by Hendrik Willem Van Loon*

ILLUSTRATED BY JAMES MAC DONALD

HARCOURT, BRACE AND COMPANY
NEW YORK

Republished by Omnigraphics • Penobscot Building • Detroit • 1992

COPYRIGHT, 1939, BY
HARCOURT, BRACE AND COMPANY, INC.

Library of Congress Cataloging-in-Publication Data
Augur, Helen.
    The book of fairs/by Helen Augur: with an introduction by
Hendrik Willem Van Loon; illustrated by James MacDonald.
      p.   cm.
    Reprint. Originally published: New York: Harcourt, Brace, c1939.
    ISBN 1-55888-892-6 (lib. bdg.: alk. paper)
    1. Fairs—History. I. Title.
HF5471.A8   1990
381'.18—dc20   89-29244
                                                                                    CIP

∞

This book is printed on acid-free paper meeting the ANSI Z39.48 Standard. The infinity symbol that appears above indicates that the paper in this book meets that standard.

Printed in the United States of America

To W. C. M.

TABLE OF CONTENTS

1. Fairs Before History — 3
Primitive fairs and festival fairs from 2000 B.C.

2. Joyous Cities — 28
Tyre, sixth century B.C.; Athens, fifth century B.C.

3. The Roman World — 55
Rome, 500 B.C. to 476 A.D.

4. Voyage to Cathay — 82
Venice and the Chinese fair of Kinsai, late thirteenth century

5. Jean Goes to Champagne — 107
French fairs, late thirteenth century

6. New Goods and New Places — 136
Flanders and Germany, fifteenth century

7. English Variety — 157
Ancient fairs; Stourbridge and Bartholomew, seventeenth century

8. West Meets East — 188
Nizhni Novgorod, Russia, nineteenth century

9. The Machine Age — 206
European expositions, 1851-1936

TABLE OF CONTENTS

10. Native American Fairs — 232
City of Mexico, 1519; American agricultural fairs

11. Growth of a Continent — 261
American world's fairs, nineteenth and twentieth centuries

12. The Pride of Cities — 281
San Francisco and New York, 1939

Index — 299

LIST OF ILLUSTRATIONS

Bruges had a genius for pageantry	frontispiece
The savages came out from hiding	23
The Great Sea in 550 B.C.	41
In Nero's time Rome was a perpetual Mardi Gras	63
Marco Polo sees the land of Kublai Khan	95
Routes to Champagne, 13th century	115
"Oyez! Oyez! The glove is up!"	167
Routes to Nizhni in 1840	191
Albert shows Victoria the Crystal Palace model	217
"Pure agricultural hoss-trots"	255
New York had a Crystal Palace too	265
Streamline and fantasy	289

INTRODUCTION

By *HENDRIK WILLEM VAN LOON*

I AM now speaking of prehistoric times—of those blessed days in the late eighties and the early nineties when nobody had ever seen a passport, when you traveled from one end of the world to the other without ever being asked one single little question about your social or racial antecedents and when you could cross and recross the same frontier ten times a week without arousing the slightest suspicion as either a smuggler or a political agitator. And I am thinking of the happiest week of the whole year in those blessed prehistoric times—of the week of the annual fair.

It was called the *Kermis*, a word that is often confused with our own Christmas, but that has nothing to do with the merry Yuletide, for it meant the annual mass celebrated in memory of the day when a particular church had been first consecrated. As those events went way back to the earliest times of the Middle Ages, when the world lived happily on a basis of complete individuality and when repentant malefactors of great wealth were apt to found a church any time their consciences bothered them into such an act of expia-

INTRODUCTION

tion, these church-fairs came at all sorts of strange dates and without the slightest regard for the convenience of the participants. Way up in the north, the good city of Groningen might celebrate its fair on May the fifteenth and Breda, at the other end of the country, might have its fair on the twelfth. Those fairs were apt to be held during an entire week and it meant that all the merchants who attended the festivities had to dismantle in a hurry, pack in a hurry, hoist all their belongings on a couple of flatcars and rush to the next place of business.

I mention this otherwise irrelevant detail because those transmigrations are among the earliest and happiest of my childhood memories. Since then I have seen the Taj Mahal and Fuji (on postal cards) and most of the other wonders of this world with mine own eyes, but none of them filled my soul with that sublime satisfaction that came from staring at a row of wooden lions or giraffes who lay in picturesque disarray on our ancient marketplace and who the next afternoon were to carry me with dizzy speed and a dizzier din around the perilous course of the first genuine "steam carousel."

The application of steam to this circular movement was then a novelty. Until then, man-power had been the exclusive motive force and if one were very fortunate, the owner would perhaps allow half a dozen of us to assist him. I am sure he had never heard of Tom Sawyer, but the system

INTRODUCTION

worked and after half an hour or so, we were sometimes given a free ride. That meant a saving of five cents, and believe me, we needed it for in those days the annual fair transformed our humble marketplace into an exact replica of those Golden Streets of which one can find all the glorious details in that volume which St. Augustine devoted to a description of the City of God.

Alas and alack, during the beginning of the twentieth century there was an end to that week of unalloyed blessedness, at least as far as those unfortunate children were concerned who lived in the bigger cities. For the juggernaut of progress had crushed the wagon of the itinerant peddler and those pleasures which formerly had been crowded together into the short space of a single week were now an everyday institution. The merchants who for almost a thousand years had brought us cloth from Switzerland and linen from the Ukraine and cutlery from Germany could no longer fight the competition from the retail stores that arose on every corner. They had been institutions known to my parents and grandparents. I remember them only vaguely for at that age the one-ring circus and the shooting galleries (where you could destroy a dozen clay pipes for a nickel if you were an expert shot) were much more important than a neat little wooden booth where grandma bought her annual supply of linen or a clock that said cuckoo twelve times at noon. And the successors to these ancient and honorable peripatetic ten-

INTRODUCTION

cent stores did not really interest us very much. The local "Belgian Bazaar with nothing over a dime" (for some obscure reason, they were always "Belgian Bazaars") took care of all our needs for cheap trinkets and rubber balls which lost their elasticity after the first rain storm.

Then we moved to the bigger city and for many years the annual country-fair disappeared from view. Once a year, on the Queen's birthday, the stately promenade of the Hague, known as the Voorhout, was lined with a few relics of ancient times and harmonica players of very uncertain artistic talent gathered in pennies while a rather dilapidated-looking Sandow broke chains with his bare fists. But it was considered rather bad form to attend these festivities. They were supposed to be held for "the common people." In the end, even the common people stayed away and went to the movies instead. The country-fair had outlived its usefulness. After a full and happy life of almost a thousand years, it gave up the ghost. That, at least, is what we thought, but now we know better. For the fair spirit, as we have since discovered, was much older than the church-fair of the Middle Ages. Mother Church, who, whatever her short-comings, has never yet been accused of lacking in wisdom, had understood that her children must occasionally have a day of respite from the worries of everyday life. That is why she continued the old Roman Saturnalia by giving them a Christian aspect and bestowing upon them the much more respectable name of

INTRODUCTION

Carnival. That is why she encouraged the church-fair as a successor to those much older regional *marts* which we can now trace back to the age when the Phoenicians were the traders who looked after all the daily needs of the people of the Mediterranean and who seem to have extended their operations as far up north as the British Channel. And history has most convincingly taught us that such primitive instincts as the desire for an annual exchange of goods combined with popular entertainments can neither be suppressed nor definitely destroyed. For, the moment you put an end to them in one form, they will crop up again under another disguise, but they will come back regardless of all royal edicts or imperial ukases or Church interdicts, for they are an integral part of that strange "communal consciousness" which only today we are beginning to recognize and to study as one of the most important moving forces in the development of our civilization.

In proof whereof, I would like to point to the universal exhibitions and the world's fairs which sprang up all over the world as soon as the small town church-fair was beginning to lose its usefulness.

The first one of the universal expositions of which I have any personal recollection was the Great Paris Fair which took place when I was seven or eight years old and which I shall always remember because it provided me with a cowboy suit which a generous aunt had brought back for me from

INTRODUCTION

Mr. Buffalo Bill's special show at that Grande Exposition Universelle. And I was told to value it, as undoubtedly it came from the last World's Fair that ever would be held.

That happened almost half a century ago and today fairs are going stronger than ever before. Indeed, they now attract their millions when five hundred years ago they were only attended by those citizens who could boast of a horse and buggy and could drive all of six miles to the nearby town or village to lay in an annual supply of spices and buy their best girls a wedding ring or a pair of glasses (any size, any strength, as long as they looked well and added a touch of dignity to the wearer's face). For, as I just so eruditely remarked, these big exhibitions seem to be part of some primitive instinct which urges man to lose himself occasionally among his fellow-men and to forget that the first of the month will soon come around and that bills cannot be put off indefinitely if one wants to keep on eating.

I am writing this because in a way I am an "accomplice before the fact." Being one of the few survivors who, from personal experience, can tell a younger generation about the last of the medieval church-fairs, and being too busy to write a book about them myself, I had for many years looked for some willing disciple who would have the courage to dig into the mountains of material about the older sort of year-marts that lay spread all over the continent of Europe and

INTRODUCTION

to explain them and to tell us what they revealed about FAIRS THROUGHOUT THE AGES. And then one day Helen Augur told me that for quite a long time she too had been bothered with a similar curiosity. The idea therefore is really hers, for I merely indulged in a few hazy speculations, whereas she actually buried herself in the public library and did something about it.

Now if she were only a literary debutante, I could arrange a sort of paper coming-out party to celebrate this event, but as she is already the mother of several other historical children, I can only play the role of an older friend who offers his younger colleague a little bouquet when she starts forth upon this new venture and who expresses his gratitude for all the trouble she has taken on our behalf and wish her good luck. The good luck will take care of itself as soon as the book shall have been published. Meanwhile, here is the bouquet.

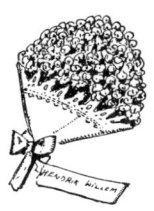

THE BOOK OF FAIRS

1

FAIRS BEFORE HISTORY

IN the spring of 1939 two magic cities, newly built on the Atlantic and Pacific coasts of America, opened their gates and invited the world to come in. The Golden Gate Exposition in San Francisco gathered up the romance of the western states with their Indian and Spanish background and their trading ties with the Orient, from the days of the clipper ships to their streamlined sisters, the China Clippers. The New

THE BOOK OF FAIRS

York World's Fair plunged into the future, and built a whole city to suggest what the world of tomorrow can be like if we combine the arts and inventions we already possess into an orderly scheme.

World's fairs like these try to sum up the accomplishments and hopes of the entire world, for most of the nations of the globe take part in them. It is an old habit for the nations to meet at fairs, so old in fact that it goes back long before history, when tribes that fought all the rest of the year would lay down their arms outside the fair ground and swear to keep the truce and deal honestly. It was in these primitive markets that our ancestors first knew peace, and this great discovery helped to build up and preserve civilization. Fairs still bring the nations together under an unspoken truce, and they still have a special atmosphere of good will and festivity that does not belong to ordinary gatherings of people.

If we follow the long fair road from the first trading civilizations to our own days, we will find fairs of many sorts performing many functions, and yet preserving the old pattern of the *peace of the fair*. There is perhaps no pleasanter road through history than the

FAIRS BEFORE HISTORY

peoples' trade route that makes detours around wars and conquests, crosses national boundaries at will, and gives us a fresh view of society and a new respect for the human race. At fairs people have always been on their best behavior. For four thousand years, no matter what dreadful things were going on outside, the fair ground itself has been a place dedicated to trade, worship, and merrymaking. These three things have always gone together in fairs, and they still do, if we take "worship" in the broad sense of human hope and wonder. When you think it over, this combination of trade, worship, and carnival is a curious one, but it is part of the history of fairs, which is downright amazing. Fairs go back farther, and have changed less, than almost any social habit. Curious as it was, their ancient pattern was so satisfactory that it changed only with methods of trade.

In the last century or so, our trading methods have changed more than in the whole time before. We are so used to railroads, planes, radios, telephones, and all the other machines that transport us or our messages, so used to having machines make what we need, that we forget that the world got along without them until a very short while back. The machine has suddenly transformed our ways of buying and selling, and this tremendous shift created our modern fairs. Up to the machine age, fairs were the heart of trade and cleared the wholesale commerce between nations; they were centers to which merchants brought goods in ships and river barges, on camels and mules, carrying back the goods exchanged for them. Until 1917, the big trade of the Russian Empire was cleared at the still medieval fair of Nizhni Novgorod, which did an annual business of more than $100,000,000. Trade now has the speed of the ether waves that carry an order from Chicago to Capetown; but trade through thousands of years was slowed down to the beat of hoofs on a road or the push of wind against sails.

In this world of slow, direct trade in which people carried goods to a place where they would meet other people carrying different goods, there is no machine in the picture, and no intricate impersonal mechanism of exchange. Commerce is now an indirect, almost invisible, thing. But commerce used to be the meeting of people who had much to exchange besides goods. They had no newspapers, so they learned the news at fairs; for a long time they had no printed books, and got ideas and what knowledge they had from meeting other people, especially at fairs. The medieval European did without many things besides machines. He had no theatres, music-halls, banks, stock exchanges, post offices, standard money, standard weights and measures, commercial law and commercial ethics, or international treaties—*except at fairs*. But the medieval fairs, especially those of Champagne, supplied their own devices to fill all these needs, and more. In fact, all these familiar institutions were first started in fairs, which experimented with them and worked them over until they were strong enough to leave the protection of the fair and develop independently. And what is more, there was only one power in feudal Europe—riding above the authorities of cities, barons, kings, and even popes—that could protect the merchant, his goods, and his rights. That power was the peace of the fair.

Our history begins here; for every fair we investigate, even those of today, bears some trace of this mysterious authority of the fair truce. We are going to search for the origin of this peace. It will take us on a voyage of exploration in which we will find one baffling and incredible thing after another, and leave many puzzles unsolved. But in the end we shall understand something of fairs and the impulse that created them.

Nobody knows when fairs began, which is another way of saying that nobody knows when trade began. The moment people began to travel some distance to exchange goods with strangers at a regular time and place, that was a fair. A market is a local affair for its own neighborhood, for the sale of food or livestock that cannot be transported far. A market is regular small trade between neighbors, a fair is regular large trade between strangers.

Regular and peaceful trade between strangers began long before civilization itself. It probably began with the need of salt, which arose when certain nomad tribes shifted from the hunting, roaming habits of the Early Stone Age and became settled people of the Late Stone Age (where we still are, in spite of our radios). The roving hunters lived on the meat they killed, and needed no salt, but the settled people began raising grains and vegetables which they could not eat without it. Like herds of buffaloes, the planters would travel long distances to find salt beds. Doubtless they began by raiding and fighting anybody who came between them and the thing they wanted, but gradually primitive men worked out ways of trading not only salt, but skins, amber, gold, and rough cloth of flax.

We know a good deal about primitive people by studying uncivilized tribes still living in many parts of the earth who have not changed along with the rest of society. We know that they are not savages continually fighting and stealing. The human race has survived in spite of war, not because of it. It has survived through its instincts of curiosity and friendliness; and these instincts, along with the strong religious motives that dominate all primitive people, led to ways of trading that were carried over into fairs. Another thing we know about primitive people is that they have no desire to "make money"—that is, to profit from trade; or to pile up wealth. They enjoy trade because it gets them the things they need for today, and because it brings them in contact with other people.

But these early men were very much afraid of each other, and so worked out curious methods of exchanging goods. One, called *silent trade,* was used all over the globe, and still is used in certain Pacific islands and in pockets of Asia and Africa. Let us say that our planter living in the fertile valley wants to exchange his surplus fruit for fresh meat from the roving herdsman. The settled tribe and the nomad tribe are continually at war, but somewhere on the boundary between farm land and grazing land there are neutral spots protected by a truce, and in these spots it is possible to trade with the enemy. Perhaps these trading sites are marked by a big tree or stone to make them safe; for all over the world, before they worshiped gods, people worshiped trees or stones.

The planter comes to a trading spot with a basket of fruit, and puts it down. He beats a drum or blows a horn as a signal, and then runs back to his side of the border and hides. For in this trading game you must not see your partner. The herdsman comes up with his fresh-killed steer, and examines the basket of fruit. If he thinks it is worth his meat, he takes the basket and leaves the meat. If not, he puts the meat beside the basket, gives his signal, and goes back into hiding. The planter comes out with more fruit, and signals again. This time the herdsman is satisfied with the trade, and takes the basket.

Here are primitive people trading with peace and honesty, but not seeing each other, perhaps because of tribal tabus about not being seen by strangers. But along with silent trade, or more probably before it, went *border trade,* in which whole tribes of strangers met on exactly such spots as we have described, neutral and sacred places on their boundaries, protected by a truce which could not be violated. It was not merely a crime to transgress the peace of these places, it was sacrilege against the spirits that lived in the tree or stone; or if god-worship had replaced magic, against the god whose image stood on this primitive fair ground. For these meetings, which took place once or twice a year, were the border fairs of the peoples who lived in the forests of Europe. Such fairs were once universal, and still survive.

Meanwhile civilizations were growing up in the warm lands around the Mediterranean, which its people called the Great Sea, never dreaming of the much greater sea beyond the western gates of their secure world. The earliest civilization of the western world was the Sumerian, which flourished more than 6,000 years ago in the traditional Garden of Eden, the fertile region where the Tigris and Euphrates empty into the Persian Gulf. The Sumerians are too far back to come into our story, but we know that they had cities with great temples of baked earth around which fairs and trade centered. And Egypt comes into ancient trade only as a placid granary that fed the restless people who explored and traded and created industry.

The commercial traditions we have inherited began with two other cultures which developed at the same time with the Egyptian—the Babylonian, and the Aegean centering in Crete and tying all the Mediterranean trade together, as Babylon tied the land trade of western Asia. About 2000 B.C. Babylon on the upper Euphrates became a great trading center for the Persians and the Semitic peoples—Arabs, Phoenicians, Syrians, and others. These Semites had traded with the old Sumerians during a long period, and had probably taken over some of their commercial methods. At any rate, by this time Babylon had a well-organized caravan trade with the countries around it, selling at its fairs grain, precious metals, wool, dates, and a great variety of products brought on the backs of men or mules. The early Levant had no horses, and camels were not used by the caravans until 1500 B.C. We will come back to these caravans and fairs later.

The Aegeans of the island civilization enjoyed perhaps the longest and happiest period of growth mankind has ever known. They were launched on the Great Sea by 4000 B.C., and for the next three thousand years were secure from invasion, and free to develop industries, arts, and trade. Their great city of Cnossos in Crete was excavated not long ago, and the old legend of King Minos and the Labyrinth came to life again, for the kings of Crete were all called Minos, and lived in a huge luxurious palace like a labyrinth. Perhaps Cnossos, wonderful as it must have been, was not the chief city of the Aegeans, who spread over Greece and the Asia Minor coast and all the islands between; but it was an important center.

On the Mediterranean sailing ships are often becalmed, so its people used rowing ships, and on long voyages always kept close to the land, the crews sleeping on shore. In their trading galleys the Aegeans wove back and forth between their sunny islands and sheltered coasts, and down to Egypt, with which Crete had long and friendly trading ties. Crete's great age was about 2500 B.C., and by this time the artisans had perfected their skill in making pottery, cloth, carved ivory and gems, metal and inlaid work, and the artists were producing paintings and sculptures. These products of art and skilled craft reached a perfection that has not so far been surpassed.

The Aegeans were gentle, luxurious people who took great delight in trade and in festivals in which their athletes competed. When we get to the Greek fairs, we will find certain elements—choral dances, wrestling and boxing matches, races—in short, all the chief features of the Greek Games and other festivals going along with fairs—which must have been taken over from the island civilization. In other words, all we know of the Aegean fairs is their resurrection in those of Greece, and in one poem of Homer describing a fair on the island of Delos that somehow preserved the old atmosphere. The language of these people has not yet been deciphered, nor their story pieced together.

We do not even know what invader destroyed this fine civilization, and burned Cnossos to the ground. The Greeks and the Phoenicians were both coming out

FAIRS BEFORE HISTORY

with fleets on the Great Sea; and both were at that time pirates and raiders. All we know is that by 1000 B.C. the Aegean civilization was ended, the Greeks were settled down in the conquered territory, and the Phoenicians were masters of the Mediterranean.

This race of supreme traders was a Semitic people who lived on a strip of the coast above Jerusalem, and who, by the time they inherited the commerce of the Great Sea, had also inherited the caravan trade of the Levant. So from now on we shall follow the Phoenicians, to whom the world is indebted for the first alphabet, for arithmetic and algebra, and for the early arts of navigation and trade. From their harbors of Tyre and Sidon they launched their ships ever further west in search of metals, and their caravans ever further east, until in the fairs of Tyre there was tin from England and cinnamon from Ceylon.

They were brave navigators, venturing along the shores of the Great Sea, adding sails to their rowing ships, and learning to steer by the North Star, and finally sailing through the Straits of Gibraltar and out into the rough Atlantic. They established a colony at Carthage on the north coast of Africa, and another in southern Spain called Tarshish. From the mines of Tarshish they got silver, copper, and iron. Then, beyond the Straits of Gibraltar they established Cadiz in southwestern Spain, and from this port they sailed south along the African coast to get gold and ivory from the black savages. There is a persistent legend that they circumnavigated Africa, trying to find a route to India. However that may be, they made regular trips up to Cornwall in southwestern England for tin. They mixed tin with the Spanish copper to make bronze, a hard alloy so useful that this whole period is called the Bronze Age. The Phoenician ships also brought back amber, which was supposed to guard the wearer from disease. And amber came only from the Baltic coast near Russia; a chain of tribal traders may have brought it to the Channel Islands or Cornwall.

The Phoenicians were just as adventurous on land, displacing Babylonians as caravan traders, surpassing Arabs and Syrians as merchants, and building up an amazing system of routes. Southward, their camel trains went to Egypt for wheat and linen, to Ethiopia for ivory and ostrich feathers, and down into Arabia the Blest, as the southern part was called, for the sacred myrrh and frankincense and pearls from the Gulf. The caravans went north for Armenian mules and horses, and slaves from Asia Minor. But the greatest push was toward "the Indies," as the East was vaguely called. Until the fourth century B.C. the Phoenicians did not get into India itself, but picked up eastern goods in Persia, to which the Indian caravans made regular trips. This merchandise was the crown of Levant trade—jewels, dyewoods, hardwoods, fine cottons, and above all, spices. The ancient world used great quantities of scents and spices, and for a long time Ceylon was called "Cinnamon Isle" as England was called "Tin Island."

These caravans were traveling cities of trade, which for long trips might include 5,000 camels; they created many fairs at oases and at the end of their routes. But caravan trade was bound up with the huge pilgrimage festivals of Egypt, Persia, and the whole ancient world. The caravans would converge, for instance, at Mabug on the Euphrates for the annual Pilgrimage to the Sea, which attracted a multitude of worshipers all the way from India to Sicily. And they would time their trips through Arabia to arrive at Mecca, a station on the incense route, for its pilgrimage festival. For the great fairs of antiquity were part of these festivals; no great religious gathering was without its fair.

It is time now to ask questions. Why did fairs go with festivals? Why does our very word fair come from the Latin *feria,* meaning festival? Why does the German word for fair, *Messe,* mean mass, the sacrament of the Church? What has buying and selling to do with religion?

We remember that Christ drove the money changers out of the temple in Jerusalem. But if we take in the whole sweep of history, Christ's anger at the money changers in the temple was the strange thing, not their presence there. Centuries before Christ was born Babylonian and Greek priests were the money changers at fairs, and Arabian priests had the sole right to sell incense. Centuries after Christ died, jugglers and acrobats as well as merchants were welcome in French cathedrals during fairs, and in England there was trading in Ely cathedral and the old St. Paul's, and the English fair crowds danced in the churches. The fairs of Europe were dedicated to Christian saints, and many of them were owned by the Church.

The usual explanation of why fairs went with festi-

FAIRS BEFORE HISTORY

vals is simple enough: the festival attracted the crowds, and the crowds attracted the traders. This is true, as far as it goes, but it does not go far enough. For there are certain mysteries to explain. For instance, there are the ancient fairs of Egypt, Greece, and Ireland, three countries which developed independent civilizations. In early Egypt, fairs were held at tombs and burial places, and the fair guard was also guardian of the tombs. In prehistoric Greece, fairs were held along with funeral games in honor of dead kings and warriors. These games, which became the Olympic and other Greek Games, continued to have fairs. The early Irish fairs were held in the burial places of kings and queens, and had funeral games like the Greek. The greatest one, the Tailte Fair, was held in midsummer like the Olympic Games, and was plainly a harvest or first fruits festival.

As Sir James Frazer points out in *The Golden Bough,* the Greek and Irish fairs were connected with worship of the dead, with games and offerings to appease the dead and get their help in persuading the gods to grant a good harvest. The only point we will make about these endlessly fascinating fairs is that they were tied to the most primitive form of religion.

THE BOOK OF FAIRS

Now let us look at the highly developed fairs of France, China, and Mexico, three countries developing without any recorded contact. The great medieval fairs of Champagne, Kinsai, and Mexico City were all "classic" fairs existing in three spots on the globe as far apart as possible, existing without the slightest knowledge of each other. And though they had fairly intricate organizations, they were all of a piece. Moreover, in the twelfth century B.C. the Rites of Chow-li, laid down by a dynasty in South China, had already gone into great detail about the layout and conduct of the classic fair. But we cannot conclude that the French, Chinese, and Aztecs of the Middle Ages were simply following the old rules. The Aztecs may have come from China carrying the Rites of Chow-li in their heads. But we shall see the French fairs growing out of their own soil, and yet developing in the same pattern as the Chinese.

This is all very mysterious: three systems of primitive fairs based on worship of the dead, and three systems of medieval fairs based on an elaborate system; all curiously alike, and yet not derived from each other. We can no more explain this than we can explain why the entire world once worshiped trees with the same rites. But we started out to find the origin of the peace of the fair, and have now pushed it so far back that it is lost in the mists that hang over the history of mankind. And that, paradoxically, is the explanation we may decide to choose.

For all these fairs, from the Olympic Games to Champagne, and all early fairs we have ever heard of, have been held under a truce that imposed upon traders a solemn pledge—spoken or unspoken—to keep the peace and to deal honestly. This truce we shall see keeping order among the warring clans of primitive Scotland, making the Phoenician who is a pirate and murderer on the seas a peaceful and honest trader at Mecca, creating among civilized people like the Chinese a tradition of peace and order on a much higher level. Fairs have always been better than the life around them; they have always been peaceful and honest.

Now, people being what they are, we can only say that if fairs make them drop their everyday characters and obey rules that are hard to follow, then fairs must have some powerful hold on human emotions, such as religion exerts. And since fairs grow up all over the world by the same pattern, no matter if this pattern gets elaborate, then we must decide that they all come from the same source. Not from the Garden of Eden or China or some other cradle of the race; but from a very deep level in the human mind in which trade is actually a part of religion. In other words, back to primitive man and his terror of offending a tree spirit or a god by committing a sacrilege.

And since it may sound fantastic to say that the peace of the fair had its origin in magic, we will repeat two stories told by the Greek historians Herodotus and Thucydides that show this magic peace working around the Great Sea in about the sixth century B.C.

Herodotus tells of Phoenician merchants from the colony of Carthage sailing down the African coast to get gold dust from the black savages. This is how they traded: The Carthaginians put a pile of goods down on the beach, rowed back to their ship, and made a fire that raised a column of smoke. At this signal, the savages came out from hiding, laid down their gold beside the goods, and vanished. The merchants came back and examined the gold, were not satisfied, and went back to their ship. So the savages brought more gold,

THE SAVAGES CAME OUT FROM HIDING

and the trade was made. Herodotus adds in some astonishment, for he had a low opinion of the Phoenicians: "Neither party ever wrongs the other; for they do not touch the gold until it is made adequate to the value of the merchandise."

In Thucydides' story, a Greek war fleet was going along the coast of its colony in Italy, trying to get recruits, and also trying to get provisions of food. The Italians were half-barbarous tribes; they did not want to send their men to war, so they shut up their town walls, and refused even to trade with the Greeks. This went on in every town until the fleet, nearly famished, got down to the tip of Italy, at Reggio.

"As they were not received within the walls, they encamped outside the city at the temple of Artemis; there they were provided by the inhabitants with a market, and drawing up their ships on shore, they took a rest."

When we remember that both the black savages and the Italian tribesmen were in great danger of being taken as slaves, we realize what implicit faith these people had in their methods of silent trade and border trade. To the Africans, the shore was a neutral and sacred spot because it separated their jungle from the merchants' sea; it may have been a trading place of long standing, or the Phoenicians may have signified the truce by setting the branch of a tree on the sand beside the goods. All savages know the symbolism of the branch, the prototype of the Christian cross. The Italians worshiped Artemis, and before her temple they were safe.

Long before this, the borders of Greece and Italy had been dotted with fair places guarded by an image of Hermes (Mercury) who was god of trade, boundaries, travelers, and fairs. The whole story is told in this combination of Hermes' special functions. Later on, the Christian cross was to stand on these same sites, which were the only ones where the tribes of Europe would meet and trade with strangers. The border fair, the oldest and most deeply rooted of all, was the type of fair that survived through the Dark Ages, when civilization collapsed with the fall of Rome. The universal border fair, which began at a time when men were friendly, and free from desire for profit, and obedient to their gods, is the first pattern of fairs and their special peace.

FAIRS BEFORE HISTORY

The fair—that part of trade which has been free from its worst sins—began with the primitive impulse to peace and honesty. Without this impulse we never would have had fairs, and probably the human race would never have survived at all.

2

JOYOUS CITIES

1. TYRE

O thou that art situate at the entry of the sea, which art a merchant of the people for many isles, thus saith the Lord God: "O Tyrus, thou hast said, 'I am of perfect beauty.' Thy borders are in the midst of the seas, thy builders have perfected thy beauty. They have made all thy ship boards of fir trees of Senir: they have taken cedars from Lebanon to make masts for thee. . . . Fine linen with broidered work from Egypt was that which thou spreadest forth to be thy sail; blue and purple from the isles of Elishah was that which covered thee. . . . The ships of Tarshish did sing of thee in

JOYOUS CITIES

thy market: and thou wast replenished, and made very glorious in the midst of the seas.

THE prophet Ezekiel, a wretched captive in Babylonia, wrote in about 593 B.C. a long lament for Tyre, which he prophesied would be destroyed along with his own country of Israel. But he could not write of Tyre without describing her fairs, so most of the lament is a rhapsody of trade. Praise of beautiful cities and ships and goods will run all through this history; Ezekiel was only the first to write of the splendors of commerce.

Sidon had been the chief city of the Phoenicians until about a thousand years before Christ, when Tyre was rebuilt by its great King Hiram, who was a friend of King Solomon. Hiram sent his skilled stonemasons and carpenters to help build the great temple in Jerusalem, and then set them to work creating the most fabulous city of the time. Old Tyre was on the mainland, but now King Hiram built New Tyre on the island which lay half a mile from the coast. The new island fortress was safe from invasion by Babylonia or Assyria, and the Tyrian fleet kept the seas secure.

King Hiram deepened the natural harbors at the

north and south of the island and made a canal to connect them, so that ships would have quiet anchorage. He enlarged the island with rubble and stone on the ocean side, and fortified it with high walls on the land side. Since the new city was now a treasure house well secured, he built there his own palace of great stone blocks roofed with cedar, and a temple to Melkart the Baal of Tyre. Near the walls were the fine houses of the merchants, four or five stories high, and set in gardens with fig and olive trees and vineyards.

Tyre's great age was at the time when Ezekiel wrote of the ships of Tarshish singing in her market. She was chief of a loose federation of the Phoenician cities, which united only in danger. Though Greece had learned enough from the Phoenicians about shipbuilding and navigation to defy her own tutors every now and then, in general the limits of each trading power were well defined. Greece had opened up the Black Sea, and its shores were hers, as were the Asia Minor coast and the African province of Libya. In the west, Greece had colonies at Marseilles, the Italian islands, and the toe of the Italian boot. Farther west she dared not go, for Tyre's colony of Carthage was now a powerful state and policed the western end of the Mediterranean. Any Greek ship caught heading for the Straits of Gibraltar was captured, and its merchants drowned.

The Phoenicians taught the Greeks many things, but certain trade secrets they kept to themselves. Neither the Greeks, nor later the Romans, could discover where the Phoenicians got their tin. The answer to torture or bribery was always, "From an island in the north." The Greeks knew that already. Finally the Gauls began bringing tin and amber down the Rhone Valley to Marseilles, so the Greeks did not have to explore the Atlantic and its unknown terrors.

The fairs of Tyre lasted a thousand years. We know little about them except for Ezekiel's long inventory of foreign merchants and goods, and some students think that Tyre had no fairs in the proper sense of the word, and that Ezekiel's phrase was merely poetic. As a matter of fact, he was so precise that he used three different Hebrew words to describe the trade that went on in Tyre: market, periodic fair, and mart. And in these three words we get a picture of trade in a city constantly full of foreign merchants, with goods constantly coming in by ships and caravans. Tyre was a

THE BOOK OF FAIRS

mart in the sense that she was always full of merchandise and traders, and that commerce was always going on—the word market shows that. The fairs would occur at religious festivals, and at times when especially big caravans arrived, and the fleet returned from Spain. When Solomon and Hiram ruled, this great event happened only once in three years. King Solomon had his own little fleet, which had probably been built in the shipyards of Sidon, and it went on these voyages with the Phoenician ships. They visited the mines of Tarshish, and the African Gold Coast, bringing back, as the Bible says, "gold, and silver, ivory, and apes, and peacocks."

As for festival fairs, they were still flourishing in the sixth century, and the Phoenician merchants made the rounds. Every Sunday, and at every new moon, the Phoenician traders put up their stalls around the temple in Jerusalem. Once a year they went to Mecca, and in other seasons to Babylon, Nineveh, whatever city was gathering a crowd of pilgrims. No doubt this world of western Asia that was knit together by caravans had its fairs in cycles, so that there were no conflicting dates. The fair circuit which the merchants ride is an important part of early systems of trade; we shall meet it again in medieval Europe and in Aztec Mexico.

Phoenicia herself was at certain seasons thronged with pilgrims who worshiped Adonis and Aphrodite (called Tammuz and Ishtar by their disciples in Babylonia and Syria) at their two principal shrines. One was at Byblus, the most ancient city of Phoenicia, and the other at Paphos on the island of Cyprus, ruled by Phoenician kings called Adonis after their god. Adonis was the corn god, or spirit of vegetation, whose annual death was mourned at midsummer festivals by throngs of lamenting pilgrims, who on the third day of the rites celebrated his resurrection. Ishtar (or Astarte or Astoreth) was the great mother goddess who loved Adonis, and who interceded with the powers of death to restore him to the earth, so that all nature might revive. The myth of Adonis, based on the yearly death and resurrection of the fields, is so universal that in Egypt he is Osiris, in Phrygia Attis, and so on around the Mediterranean.

Besides these great festivals, Tyre celebrated every year solemn rites for the Baal Melkart, who was supposed to have founded their city, and who was evidently a local variation of Adonis. His image was burned on a pyre before Hiram's temple, and his resurrection welcomed with the music of lyres, with dancing, and with the equally joyous occupations of the fair.

In her festival fairs and in her markets Tyre cleared the whole trade of the western world. In this city were gathered all the caravan goods from western Asia and the East, and all the merchandise brought by the ships crowding the two harbors. But Tyre was not merely a trading center for the goods of other countries; the products of Phoenicia herself were among the most coveted wares. This little strip of rocky coast had few natural resources besides the glorious cedars of Lebanon that crowned her mountains, but the Phoenicians took the raw materials from the rest of the world and turned them into finished goods.

By now Tyre and Sidon and the island of Cyprus were supreme in certain arts and industries. Precious metals and stones were transformed into jewelry for the luxury-loving people of the Mediterranean. They took the pearls from the Persian Gulf and Ceylon, the magic amber, the rubies of India, and set them in rings, necklaces, bracelets. Egypt had long known how to make opaque glass and beads, but the Phoenicians discovered the secret of transparent glass. They made exquisite flasks of glass colored blue, jugs shaped like animals, cups and vases decorated with lines and ribbons of color. Their potters turned out every sort of earthenware, their metal workers made plates and cups and shallow bowls of bronze, gold, and silver. These artisans had a lively sense of action, and many of their decorations tell stories of lion hunts, sieges of cities, fights between bulls and stags, the story going around in a circle with one incident following another. They drew familiar animals, birds, fish, and flowers, and legendary animals like the griffin and sphinx.

The Tyrians claimed that their god Melkart taught them their art of dyeing, and nobody disputed the story. For three thousand years "Tyrian purple" made the robes of kings, the curtains of temples, and the dresses of rich women. This royal color came from the body of the murex, a shellfish found on various coasts. The gorgeous red-violet reserved for the noblest uses came from the Tyrian shores; the Greek murex was purple without the red tinge, and that from the Atlantic almost black.

China was still unknown, which means that silk was unknown. The weavers and dyers used cotton from Egypt and Persia, linen from Egypt, and wool from Arabia and near-by Syria, which was the best. These Syrian sheep, according to Herodotus, had tails so long and heavy that they were bruised by dragging on the ground, so the shepherds tied little carts to the sheep to hold up their tails. There is nothing against believing this charming story, for long afterwards Marco Polo found sheep on the edge of Persia that had tails weighing thirty pounds. Marco Polo said nothing about little carts, but many travelers since have reported these curious sheep.

The foreign merchandise was catalogued by Ezekiel in language like this:

"Javan, Tubal, and Meshech, they were thy merchants; they traded in the persons of men and vessels of brass in thy market. They of the house of Togarmah traded in thy fairs with horses and horsemen and mules . . . Syria was thy merchant by reason of the multitude of the wares of thy making; they traded in thy fairs with emeralds, purple and broidered work, and fine linen, and coral, and agate."

JOYOUS CITIES

This means: slaves and brass utensils from the Greek colonies in Asia Minor; Armenian mules and horses; Eastern goods brought in through Damascus in Syria, the starting point for the heavy caravan trade, in exchange for the multitude of Phoenician wares. Most of this trade was still barter, though the first gold coins had just been minted by King Croesus of Lydia. Ezekiel's list is long, and builds up a picture of a great luxury fair, and of Tyre as the symbol of richness and beauty. Since all great fair towns are divided into separate markets for each class of goods, we can assume that each important trading country had its own houses where its merchants lived, its storehouses, and its section of the fair.

For instance, there would be a noisy market for livestock, and another for grain. Cloth and garments would be an important section, precious metals and jewels would probably be sold in the merchants' houses, not in the market stalls. There would be a section devoted to the pleasures of smell, in which the old world took much more delight than we do nowadays: the sacred myrrh and frankincense from Arabia, other incense and perfumes from the East, sandalwood and other fragrant woods, and spices in great bales, every spice on earth. And some part of the fair must have looked like a nursery, for the Phoenicians brought to the Mediterranean many of its beautiful trees. The palm itself, the pomegranate, and the cypress, were imported from the East as seedlings on the backs of camels.

Luxurious Tyre sold her purple robes and golden cups to all those rich people around the Great Sea who lived on the work of slaves and the poverty of peasants and artisans. There is a sentence in Isaiah's prophecy of Tyre's coming doom, made three centuries before Ezekiel's, which shows his feeling, rare enough in those days, that the goods of the world were not fairly divided. "And her merchandise . . . shall not be treasured or laid up; for her merchandise shall be for them that dwell before the Lord, to eat sufficiently, and for durable clothing."

But Isaiah, too, felt the magic of Tyre. In his prophecy which begins, "Howl, ye ships of Tarshish," he cries:

Howl, ye inhabitants of the isle.
Is this your joyous city
Whose antiquity is of ancient days?

JOYOUS CITIES

Who hath taken this counsel against Tyre, the crowning city,
Whose merchants are princes,
Whose traffickers are the honorable of the earth?

But doom did not come upon the joyous city for a long time. Just after Ezekiel's prophecy, Tyre stood a fourteen years' siege by Babylonia, and her destruction was finally accomplished by Alexander the Great in 332 B.C. But meanwhile Athens had inherited her place as chief trader of the Great Sea.

2. ATHENS

History played rather a joke on Athens when it appointed her merchant of the Mediterranean. Greece had little overland trade, so her traffic was on the water; and the Greeks rather feared the sea, and were not natural traders. Yet by the middle of the fifth century B.C. Athens had become the world's emporium. This was the Golden Age of Pericles, who helped commerce by improving Athens' harbor, the Piraeus, and who put the future in his debt by building the Parthenon in honor of the goddess Athena.

The trade that supported the shining brief period of Athens' greatness was based on what the ships could bring home from the colonies. That meant chiefly that Greece got luxuries from her factories at Syracuse in Sicily, and wheat and slaves from the Black Sea region. She sold as many slaves as she could spare to other countries, and a third of her wheat. The rest was consumed at home, for the soil was too poor to feed the people, though it produced a surplus of wine and olive oil for export. In industry Athens had hardly developed beyond little home factories with two or three workers.

When the half-barbaric Greeks settled down upon the ruined Aegean culture, they absorbed many of its elements very quickly, for within three centuries they were writing their history in the epics of Homer. But it took them a long time to learn peaceful ways of trade, and they never had the passion for it which the Aegeans had displayed. To the Greek, trade for a long time meant piracy, which was a perfectly respectable way to earn a living quickly. Between the Phoenicians and the Greeks, the Great Sea was a raiding field almost to the Golden Age. Finally a King Minos, who lived in his ruined city, managed to clear the pirates out. Greece won her war with the Persians, and settled down to nearly a century of quiet.

THE GREAT SEA IN 550 B.C.

JOYOUS CITIES

But Golden Age Greece was a divided country, a mass of islands and a mainland cut by mountains; and she was divided as a nation. In fact, she was not a nation at all, but a loose league of city-states that sometimes fought each other. Under Pericles Athens was so powerful through her trade that she held the rest of the country together. Like the other city-states, Athens had shuffled off her kings and had a republican form of government. It was not a democracy, for its control rested in the small class of "citizens," those fortunates whose parents had been born in Athens. Only citizens could vote or own property; everybody else, even a rich man from the nearest town, was an "alien." It was these aliens who ran the trade that made the citizens rich. Below these two classes were the serfs and slaves, in other words, the people who worked. During this period the freedmen and the slaves dressed and lived much alike.

The age was golden. Pericles, the wise statesman, discussed sculpture with Phidias, history with Herodotus, philosophy with Socrates, and poetry with Euripides. But Athens bought her patrician leisure by keeping under heel all the aliens, all the common people, and all the women. No freeborn Athenian woman was allowed to leave her own part of the house except during the festival fairs. She stayed indoors weaving cloth and making shoes and clothes with the slaves; and when the cloth was finished, the slave woman took it to market to sell, and the free woman stayed a prisoner. In any household too poor to own a slave, the husband had to do the daily marketing.

Still, fresh garlands were sold in the Athens market. When a market sells fragrant wreaths and roses, ribbons, singing birds and pet dogs, and dolls and balls for the children, it means a joyous city. The people were poor, but much better off than they had been; the whole city was in a period of new prosperity and confidence. There was something golden in Pericles' Athens, even for the women forever shut away and for the peasants up in the stony hills. Poetry was in the air, and music. The people had glorious bodies, for the Greek Games had made them a nation of athletes. They had discarded the flowing Ionian garments of the islands for the short white wool chiton we see in the classic sculptures.

The market or agora was in the center of town, a

bargaining bedlam kept in order by the Clerks of the Market, who kept prices within a fair range and collected stall rents. Athens had worked out a system for running markets and fairs and taxing their sales, and another system for foreign trade. A small retail trade went on in the shops around the agora, and a small business of pressing olive oil and making pottery.

The wholesale and foreign trade of the city-state centered in the Piraeus, which was a busy emporium where the aliens and the other foreigners lived and traded. Here came the Greek grain ships from the Black Sea; the luxury ships from the Greek port of Miletus in Asia Minor or from Tyre, bringing the eastern caravan goods; and others bringing linen from friendly Egypt or carpets and furniture from Syracuse. These ships were getting big now, some of them were 250 tons, and made between five and six knots.

The finest luxury goods were stored away to be sold at fairs, and the Piraeus was chiefly occupied with the grain trade and with shipbuilding, both strictly regulated. Athens had secured a monopoly of the hard wood and metals for building ships, and forced the other Greek cities to sell these materials solely in the Piraeus.

THE BOOK OF FAIRS

Greece was burning her forests fast to make charcoal, so most of the wood came from the Indies, Sicily, and Crete, where the imported cypress flourished.

The Piraeus had its own cosmopolitan life, and its own festivals. Plato begins his *Republic* with a typical Piraeus scene in which Socrates and his disciples run into a festival for the goddess Artemis. In the afternoon there was a ceremonial procession followed by prayers to the goddess, in the evening a new sensation—a horse race in which the riders passed a blazing torch from hand to hand.

Classic Greece was incandescent with festivals to the gods, and fairs went along with them. These celebrations were escapes, quite literally, for the suppressed part of the country. For during these ceremonies alone the slaves were allowed to act like free men, the prisoners were let out of jail, and the women were allowed to attend and even take part in some of the rites.

Trade at the fairs was by tradition confined to the best and costliest wares, for knick-knacks and trash did not belong in these beautiful festivals. The choicest glass and pottery from Tyre and Sidon, and their stuffs of royal purple, perfumes, incense, rare spices, medicinal roots and herbs, the most cunning work of the armorer, potter, and goldsmith, the fabulous carpets of Persia, and the comeliest women slaves—these treasures were reserved for sale at the fairs. In the fair goods we get back the opulence of Tyre and of Cnossos, which seems almost out of place among these classic figures in their straight undyed chitons and fresh garlands. But the Greeks were not all plain livers and high thinkers like Socrates, and there was so much demand for luxuries that the fairs were held in certain places each year, though some of the festivals themselves occurred only at four year intervals.

We cannot begin to make a list of these Fairs of the Gods. They went along with the Isthmian, Olympic, Nemean, and Pythian Games, with the feasts of Isis at Tithorea every spring and autumn, with the Feast of the Hecatombs at Argos, the panegyrics at Athens, the Hyacinthine rites at Sparta. Many of the smaller towns had fairs, and along the borders ran the chain of trading sites protected by Hermes.

But it was not only these boundary fairs which were held under a truce. At the great festivals, not only was the whole region around the fair held under its sacred peace, but in effect the whole of Greece was put under a truce. The city-states renewed their oaths of peace with other cities or with foreign nations at these times. The festivals were held in such veneration that whenever two Greek cities started a quarrel, their first move was to forbid each other the freedom of their fairs, a supreme affront. Such a crowning insult to the city of Megara by Athens started the civil wars that finally overthrew her.

The civil systems which the cities had built up to regulate ordinary trade were in the fairs made subordinate to the priests, who supervised this almost ritual commerce in precious wares. The priests were the money changers for the fairs, a crucial task in this period when money was so unstandardized that it was often bought and sold as a commodity with no fixed value. The priests were also embryo bankers, lending money to responsible merchants. The peace of the fair was strictly kept. Anybody committing even a minor offense was far more severely punished than if he had committed the same offense at an ordinary time. The Clerks of the Market were required to keep order in the fairs, and at these times they carried whips, and punished offenders on the spot—a sight seen only at fairs, and rarely enough then. All debts and obligations incurred at fairs were considered sacred.

But a motley crew is invading the solemn peace of the fair, mocking it, defying the Clerks to use their whips, and the priests to banish them. Here come the jugglers with their bright shower of balls from the right hand to the left, the artists of the rope, the fortune tellers, the animal trainers, and the clowns. Here are the eternal vagrants, the peddlers of fun, as old, probably, as the fair itself, as old as the pilgrimages to Mecca and its incense trade, the oases of nonsense in the long caravan routes. Now that the Olympic Games have started history with dates, the carnival makers can bow and set to work. But they have been in the background all this time, and from now on we shall see them on every road leading to a fair.

Pericles himself could not have forbidden them their part in the official festival of his city-state to its patroness Athena. Phidias had made a colossal statue of the goddess on the Parthenon, and every four years the townspeople wove a new robe of white wool for Athena, and carried it up to her. The robe was so vast that it was stretched on the masts of a great ship built on rollers, which headed the procession through the streets and up to the Parthenon. After it came the droves of sheep and oxen for the sacrifice, maidens carrying libation bowls, youths with flutes and lyres, chariots and horsemen, and the whole population of the city-state. This superb procession has been preserved in the Parthenon frieze, now in the British Museum.

The Greek Games not only preserved the memory of the ancient funeral games, but they tied the country together in a common enthusiasm. The first Olympiad was in 776 B.C., beginning history as we know it, and the games went on for a thousand years. There were four systems of games, but the best were the Isthmian at Corinth and the Olympic. The modern world has revived them and tried to copy their perfection. But we cannot copy the picture of the judge in his laurel wreath and Tyrian purple crowning the victor of the great five point contest with a circlet of olive. The wreath was all the Olympic victor got, but for the next four years he was the greatest man in Greece, and when he drove home from the games in his chariot, his town often tore down part of its walls to make a path for the victor and the shouting crowds.

It is in the festival fairs of Delphi and the island of Delos, in honor of Apollo, dearest of the Greek gods, that we recapture the spirit of the old Aegean peoples. Apollo himself was said to have led the Cretans, at the time their island was invaded, to Delphi, center of the Greek earth. There he killed the great dragon or python that guarded the entrance to the underworld; there at his shrine the Pythoness, the priestess who now spoke for the dead Apollo, went into her sacred frenzies and told kings and generals and humble pilgrims the mind of the god about their future; and there, every four years, was the great festival of the Pylaia—the people's name for fair.

The shrines of Apollo at Delphi and Delos were treasure houses of valuables that the people confided to the keeping of the god. In order to protect these shrines there grew up the League of Neighbors (Amphictyonies) which met every year at these shrines during the fairs. The League had representatives from the chief states of Greece, and in a sense was the only national body. But it was not political; it was a league for peace. Safety for the pilgrims on the roads and on the seas, peace during festivals, and a sworn truce between themselves, an effort to make wars more humane, and a hope that wars might some day cease altogether—such were the functions and the objectives of the League of Neighbors.

The Delos fairs carry us back still further to the gracious days of Crete, for Delos was one of the islands in which there lingered the old gentle ways. When Homer visited Delos about three centuries after Cnossos had been destroyed, he found the people still wearing their flowing Ionian robes, and still loving luxury and peaceful trade among the islands. There was magic in Delos, the birthplace of Apollo, whose shrine was sheltered by the first palm brought west by the Phoenicians. It was still growing in the Golden Age, and Euripides called it Greece's "first-born palm." Homer saw it in its youth, and makes Odysseus exclaim, when he sees the lovely maiden Nausicaa, "Never have mine eyes beheld such an one among mortals, neither man nor woman; great awe comes upon me as I look on thee. Yet in Delos once I saw as goodly a thing: a young sapling of a palm tree springing by the altar of Apollo."

But Homer saw also a festival fair at Delos, when

all the people of the islands loaded their galleys with rich wares and came to buy and sell, to sing and dance to Apollo. To the poet the people themselves seemed godlike and eternally young. Here the worshipers offered their most precious goods, and watched the young men in their ritual games, and listened to the chorus

of Delian maidens exalt Apollo, then Leto and Artemis, "then sing in memory of the men and women of old time, enchanting the tribes of mortals." We should like to have heard that song of the people of old time, but that world had vanished, and we have only a glimpse of a beauty forever lost that lived again for a moment in the Delos fair:

"Apollo, thy greatest joy is in Delos, where are gathered together the Ionians in flowing robes, with their wives and children in thy street; there do they delight thee with boxing and dancing and song. Who so en-

THE BOOK OF FAIRS

countered them would say they are exempt from old age and death, beholding them so gracious, and would be glad at heart, looking on the men and fair-girdled women, and their much wealth, and their swift galleys." *

* Homer, *Hymn to Apollo*.

3

THE ROMAN WORLD

ROME, according to the familiar legend, was founded by Romulus and Remus, orphans mothered by a wolf. While there is a wolfish quality in Rome's history, the legend is no longer believed. In reality, Rome was founded on a fair ground. There was a ford on the Tiber River where the Latins from the south and east and the Etruscans from north of the river used to meet and trade in a border fair, and around this ford the city grew up.

The Latins were Aryan tribes which had come down from the north and settled Italy before 1000 B.C. The Etruscans were evidently Aegeans who fled from the Greek islands at this same period, when Cnossos was destroyed. They drove the Latins out of the northern part of Italy as far as the Tiber, and settled down to produce beautiful pottery and metal work as they had at home, trading them to the half-civilized Latins at the ford. Gradually this spot was settled by traders, and refugees from the Latin townships, who were safe on the sacred ground of the trading post. Rome thus started in a tradition of peace, which was immediately broken by a series of wars between Latins and Etruscans for possession of the city, which the Latins finally won in the sixth century B.C.

Within two centuries more the Roman Republic ruled central Italy, and the fine Etruscan culture was plowed under. Literally plowed under, for even today some peasant will turn up another piece of Etruscan sculpture or pottery to enrich the Italian art galleries. But the Graeco-Etruscan influence lingered in the people and their festival fairs, and fresh streams

THE ROMAN WORLD

from Greece were forever pouring into Italy and shaping her festivals. From very early times Italy and her islands had been granaries and victualing stations for the Greek fleet, and Syracuse was an important colony. And even when imperial Rome had made Greece a colony, she still had an inferiority complex—and quite rightly—about the older culture, and eagerly seized on the Greek gods, games, arts, or anything that would lend grace and authority to her official festivals.

To find the history of fairs from the most primitive times up to the Middle Ages, we have only to dig down into the foundations of Rome, for everything is here. Rome, which even less than Greece respected trade, which had so little understanding of human institutions that it almost extinguished fairs, nevertheless molded their traditions into laws. This is one of the accidents of history, for Rome had no sympathy for the fair pattern of peace and brotherhood. She followed another pattern altogether—conquest and easy money got from conquest. But the long roads and fine bridges she built for her warring legions were useful to merchants on their way to fairs; and her genius for setting things down in laws meant that the old religious peace of the fair gradually turned into the modern laws of commerce.

The whole story of the skyrocketing and collapse of Rome is the story of a power machine trying to ride over the needs and will of the common people. Eventually the people got back the fairs that they needed and wanted, and got them back with interest. The great days of fairs are still ahead. But for a thousand years they had to exist as well as they could under the power machine.

At the beginning of this period, when the Latins conquered Rome, primitive fairs flourished all over the western world. A thousand years later they were still flourishing, and Rome had changed them very little. This basic fair, which combines religion, trade, and carnival, meets the needs of people in a simple state of civilization, and people of this kind lived all over what was to become the Roman Empire. There were border fairs between Gauls and Italians or Germans, primitive festival fairs for the people of Egypt or Ireland. And these ancient fairs continued to run straight along beside newer types developed by Rome, for her own neighborhood. Imperial Rome made no attempt to

THE ROMAN WORLD

change the habits of her colonies up on the borders of Scotland or down near Jerusalem; she merely built a road nearly four thousand miles long to connect Scotland with Jerusalem.

The Roman Republic began by renovating the ancient festival fairs in its own vicinity. One, called the Latin Fair (*Feria Latina*), probably had the longest life of any Greek or Roman festival, for it began long before there was a settlement at the Tiber ford, and lasted almost until the Roman Empire fell. Its foundations were laid deep in the kinship of the Latin tribes, who lived a simple pastoral life, and worshiped Jupiter upon the Alban Hill. When we say the Latins worshiped Jupiter we are using a new name for an old god, perhaps the Greek Zeus of the Etruscans across the Tiber, but probably an older god still.

Every year the tribes met on the Alban Hill above the trading ford to renew their alliance before the altar of Jupiter. They offered their god a libation of milk instead of wine, for as yet there were no vineyards in the country. Then a pure white heifer which had never known the yoke was sacrificed. The flesh was roasted and eaten by the Latin deputies as a sort of communion and symbol of their brotherhood. Then there was a general carnival and fair.

The Republic continued to hold the Latin Fair every April on the Alban Hill, and renewed the alliance between Rome and the other Latin cities at this festival, which was held under a solemn truce. The consuls of the Republic were required to attend the ceremonies and offer the libation of milk. Later a second festival to Jupiter was added in the Roman Games early in September. The last three days of this fortnight's festival were devoted to the fair. This was also true of the Apollan Games and the Plebeian Games, which were set up about 200 B.C. around the nucleus of ancient fairs.

Apollo had been taken over from Greece, and his games, which were held the second week in July, had from the first a Greek flavor. There were chariot races and scenic shows as in Delphi and Delos. The Italians had also taken over Apollo's twin sister Artemis, whom they called Diana. She was a harvest goddess, and her festival came in mid-August after the slaves had gathered the crops, and they were allowed to go to her beautiful old temple on the Aventine Hill for the ceremonials. She was the special protectress of slaves, and if they ran away from their masters, they were safe in her temple.

The slaves had another friend in the old Latin goddess of fairs and harvest, Feronia, around whom the Republic built the Plebeian Games. By this time most of the plebeians were the descendants of freed slaves, and Feronia was loved by all the suppressed people of the state. She had sacred groves in which the people of central Italy had long held fairs, and a temple at Terracina devoted to the manumission of slaves. But she had never belonged to Romans until the Republic made her a patroness of the Plebeian Games, which were held the first two weeks of November.

One more festival held trade and religion together during the Republic, the fair on May 15 for Mercury, god of trade. Like his father Jupiter, Mercury may be the Latin version of a Greek god, but more probably he is as old as Hermes himself. Otherwise, it would be difficult to explain certain things about his cult in Rome, and even more difficult to explain how images of Mercury spread very early over Europe and the British Isles. At any rate, his first temple in Rome was built with its first houses, and the merchants celebrated his festival there every year.

The Republic, and later the Empire, admitted the people free to their official games. It was considered the duty of the state to keep up religious festivals. But Rome tended to separate trade from religion, and took over only those old fairs that were so precious to the people that it dared not do otherwise. Already new official festivals which had no fairs were growing up, and by the time of Nero Rome was a perpetual Mardi Gras, but in that turbulent city fairs had disappeared. So had the peace of the simple people who had worshiped the Jupiter of the tribes, Apollo and Diana, the merciful Feronia, and Mercury, on whose trading grounds no blood could be shed.

But before Rome became an empire and abandoned the simple and often fine traditions of its people, the Republic transformed two other types of fairs which are peculiar to Italy. These native fairs are probably not as old as the festival fairs, but they stretch back before history.

The first type, the *nundinae,* are important because out of them grew our laws of commerce. These fairs,

IN NERO'S TIME ROME WAS A PERPETUAL MARDI GRAS

by the time of the Republic, were held in the chief Italian cities and in Rome, and they are comically Roman. The Romans were superstitious about dates, and their calendar was littered with days that were lucky and days when nothing important could be done without disaster. The calendar revolved around the *nundinae*. The word comes from the Latin *nine*, for the fairs occurred every ninth day—that is, if you count twice over the holiday that ends one week and begins the next, as the Romans did. Actually, they had an eight day week, divided into seven rustic days when everybody worked in the fields, and one fair day when everybody came to town to bathe, rest, hear the news, trade, attend political meetings, settle legal affairs, and have little celebrations with family and friends.

The *nundinae* were dedicated to Jupiter or Saturn, but were not holy days. They had to be shifted now and then so that they would not fall on positively unlucky days; and with their calendar always jumping about, the people found it convenient to reckon time by the *nundinae*. For instance, voting came three *nundinae* after a political meeting. These holidays were of course the center of community life, rather like the combined Saturday and Sunday of country life nowadays. And Rome and the cities at this period were not so different from the market towns where our farmers gather when the week's work is done to transact their business and see their friends.

The trading at the fairs was simple enough—the exchange of salt and country produce for cloth and manufactured goods and a few luxuries that came from Carthage, Sicily, or Greece. There was not much money coined, and trade was often in the form of direct barter. Until Rome and the other cities grew large enough to need daily markets, all goods were exchanged at the *nundinae*.

Like Greece, Rome developed a system for preserving the peace of the fair. Very early in each town there was a magistrate with the title of edile who had charge of trade and public games, and was helped by two, and later four, minor ediles. This magistrate kept order at fairs, saw that transactions were honest, and inspected weights and measures. The ediles were especially strict about the sale of livestock or slaves because of the possibility of these animals—as beasts and slaves were regarded—having hidden flaws that the seller might conceal. He was required to attach a true pedigree to each slave, and repeat it verbally at the time of sale. If he misrepresented things, he was liable to a fine twice the purchase price.

Roman commercial law was based on the *jus nundinarum*, or Fair Law, which was nothing in the world but the peace of the fair carried over into law books. The Fair Law was based on the two eternal principles of peace and honesty in trade, which primitive people all over the world had established. At first, any crime of violence or cheating was considered a crime against the peace of the fair, but gradually these offenses were considered as crimes against the state itself. The state now took over the function that had belonged to a god—the safeguarding of people who come to fairs, and of their goods. Finally, in the last days of the Roman Empire, the old Fair Law was set down in a legal code which provided protection for all people coming to markets and fairs. Goods could not be seized or merchants arrested in a fair or market for debts incurred or crimes committed elsewhere. This principle of fair sanctuary persisted almost to modern times.

THE BOOK OF FAIRS

The *nundinae* were town fairs, and the other old system of native fairs called market councils (*fora et conciliabule*) belonged to the remote parts of Italy and Gaul outside of towns. In fact, towns which became large cities grew up later on the sites of these market councils which for a long time took the place of towns. These sites were as a rule old shrines and temples to which the whole population of the district went for festivals and trade. But as time went on and life became more settled, the festival fairs took on many aspects of town life. Along with religious rites and trading went the community councils which elected magistrates, administered justice, levied troops, and in general carried on all the affairs of the people in the district. Like the *nundinae,* the market councils were fairs plus, for besides the usual trade and worship they took in the legal and political activities of the people. Not only did many great cities of Italy and France grow up around the market councils, but they contained the germ of city government.

These native fairs died down as the cities grew large enough to need daily markets. Markets were called forums, and Rome eventually had special forums for each class of goods—one for livestock, another for wine, another for fish, and so on. These forums, like all markets, were gathering places for the townspeople, and took on such political importance that nowadays "forum" means free-for-all discussion, and its old connection with the sale of cheese and slaves is forgotten. Rome and the other cities also developed retail trade in shops, and as the country got rich the forums and shops became a glittering part of the general luxury.

By the time the Empire was established the old fairs had disappeared in all but the distant corners of Italy. In early Rome the edile in charge of fairs really regulated all commerce, but now he did little but oversee contracts made at markets. The control of fairs and festivals went to a prefect who had charge of the public peace, and the peace of the fair was extended into laws covering commerce in general.

In fact, the old fair system had been so suffocated that the Empire tried to revive dead fairs and create new ones, especially outside of Rome, where trade was without its accustomed outlets. All sorts of laws, including that of eminent domain, grew out of Rome's attempt to get its fair system working. The state now decided that it owned the fairs, which was a new idea. Before this, nobody had owned fairs; the land they occupied was neutral and also sacred as belonging to Mercury or some other god. But the state now set down the principle of law that the right to maintain fairs or create new ones belonged to the government (and later on, to the Emperor alone). So now the state was able to grant towns or rich landowners the right to hold fairs, which meant that the state could get a revenue out of fairs; another new idea. Some fairs were exempt from taxation, but there were duties on markets, merchants, and sales, and of course on goods coming in from other countries.

The Empire succeeded in making fairs profitable to itself, and in separating them from the old traditions. Traders now kept the peace not in fear of the god but in fear of the edile who enforced the *Pax Romana*. From now on, the fair was split up. The carnival and religious elements went their way through the dreadful chapter of circuses and gladiatorial shows dedicated to the gods; and trade went its way alone, dishonored too by Rome's mania for profits. When Rome was finished, the fair became a triple institution again in the new form given it by the Catholic Church, though underneath it was still the old pagan fair.

The fate of the fair is a symbol of what happens when a power machine gets started. The Empire began in 146 B.C., but the power machine began its mischief more than a century before in the senseless war with Carthage. After the destruction of Tyre by Alexander the Great, her colony Carthage became the chief trader of the Mediterranean and the guardian of its peace. Rome was neither, but she was afraid of Carthage, and when that city tried to root out some freebooting pirates who had taken refuge on Italian soil, Rome sided with the pirates. And thus the Punic Wars began. When they ended, the splendid trading cities of Carthage and Corinth had been brutally destroyed, and the centers of trade now became Constantinople and Alexandria.

Rome lost her soul in winning the wars. She had been a poor agricultural country with nothing much to export, and so had lived simply and on the whole honorably. Now she was suddenly rich with loot and tribute and slaves, and she went mad for more conquest and more riches. From now on the history of

THE BOOK OF FAIRS

Rome makes no more sense than a nightmare. Easy money ruined the Empire, and set back for centuries the growth of civilization.

A new class of shrewd men rode up with the tide and became rich, while the patricians and plebeians with their old Latin virtues became poorer and poorer. Slaves increased until they made up more than half the population. Banking and the new idea of credit grew up like mushrooms. Everybody, even peasants, began speculating and borrowing and hoping for more conquests to settle the score. The conquests were forthcoming, and by the time Julius Caesar was dead, Rome was master of the Mediterranean countries and of Gaul and Britain. Tyre and Sidon as part of Syria were Roman subjects; so were Greece and Egypt and Carthage and Spain.

In Rome, the Emperor Augustus, rejoicing in his new title of Pontifex Maximus, watched slaves captured from Britain trampled to death by elephants captured from Africa, while history shifted from the old to the new era with the birth of Christ in a Roman colony. The Roman calendar did not change, nor the Roman habits; presently Christians were trampled to death in

THE ROMAN WORLD

Rome. It was more than three centuries before another emperor, Constantine, asked forgiveness on his deathbed for the crimes of his country against the Christians.

Rome was now so reeking with money that the only problem was how to spend it. The state spent its easy money in an orgy of building and public games, and the rich citizens spent theirs trying to become gentlemen. This spending period comes into the history of fairs because, vulgar and confused as it was, it helped communications and built up commerce, and incidentally kept alive the wandering bands of fair entertainers.

All over her empire Rome built circuses, theatres, baths, temples, triumphal arches—and roads. By now there was a multitude of cities in the Empire, and tribute to be collected, and the *Pax Romana* to be enforced by the legions. So Rome built her wonderful roads. The longest one started up near Edinburgh, and with links across seas, went through York, London, Rheims, Lyons, Milan, Rome, Brindisi, Constantinople, Antioch, Tyre, and finally stopped at Jerusalem. The Roman roads cut straight as a sword thrust from city to city; they were laid on sand, gravel, and cement, and paved with stones or granite; they were accurately marked with mileposts; and they had relay stations with a big stable of horses every few miles. The Roman relay post was so rapid that the riders made a hundred miles a day. Though the great roads fell into disrepair after Rome collapsed, many of them were mended and are still used.

As for state spending in public amusements, it ended in debauching the entire population. The people were restless and unhappy, and the state tried to keep them quiet with a little bread and many circuses, until finally there were 175 holidays in the year, and the people were more miserable than ever. It is possible that they were not really cheered up by the sight of gladiators maiming and killing each other, or slaves being torn to pieces by African lions. They seemed to prefer the horse and chariot races and the performances of skilled entertainers, as in the days before Rome got so rich. In fact, the common people liked the same carnival amusements that crowds do today.

We know the names now of some of the old Roman entertainers—Mastex the knife thrower, who could plant knives between the outspread fingers of his sister who stood against a wall an incredible distance away; Ventilator the supreme juggler; Senex the contortionist sheathed in African snakeskins; and Funambulus the tight rope artist, who would stroll to the middle of his rope, take off his tunic and play ball with it, put it on again, and finish his walk. These entertainers were public idols.

There were trained elephants and dancing bears, magicians and wrestlers, marionette shows and teams of young Greek dancers. One popular feat of these dancers was to whirl around on a big wheel while they wrote messages on tablets and tossed them to the audience. The crowds of Rome liked the athletes and entertainers from Greece, Greek plays, and pantomimes. But most of the carnival artists during the Empire were not Greek; they had come from Asia in groups and caravans, drifted into Egypt, and so to Rome.

Who were these carnival people, the eternal nomads of the side show, and where did they come from? From India, so they said; and certainly Mastex, the knife thrower, and the necromancers and magicians were Indian. Fairs in India have always been rich and important, and perhaps these nomads were part of the surplus goods that India was always sending west. Like the gypsies, who came into fairs later, we can only say that the carnival people in Rome came from nowhere and went everywhere, and that in the course of their wanderings they picked up the arts of magic and of amusing crowds, which is a sort of magic.

Roman spending kept alive the carnival artists who somehow weathered the Dark Ages and reappeared with their old bags of tricks in the fairs of Europe. And Roman spending kept alive the luxury trade of the world. The rich citizens of the first two centuries of our era were interested only in buying things when, as Mr. H. G. Wells complains, they should have been spending this period of comparative peace and quieter manners in learning about their empire. But the citizens were lazy. They took no interest in geography or science or in the fine works of their own poets and dramatists. It was so much simpler to buy a learned Greek slave to recite the classics while the master drank Greek wine and played with a pet leopard. Another learned slave—for most of the physicians were slaves —would take care of him if he drank too much wine.

The Roman matron who wore a robe of purple silk

knew only that a pound of silk cost a pound of gold. She never dreamed that the silk was spun by worms in northern China, carried on a camel through Chinese Turkestan and down the Valley of the Indus to Karachi, then by ship, caravan, and Nile boat to Alexandria, where it was dipped twice in Tyrian dye and shipped to a shop in Rome. We cannot blame the Roman matron for not knowing that worms made her silk robe, for this was the most colossal trade secret in history, locked behind the Great Wall of China. The point is that she wouldn't even have been interested if somebody had told her about the intricate network of trade and the sheer human toil involved in her banquet finery. She missed all the romance behind her tortoise-shell combs from India, her amber, that had passed from hand to hand across the whole of Europe, and her perfume from Arabia the Blest. All she knew was that things cost too much, and she was right about that, for the Roman merchants were getting very rich.

The merchants were just as indifferent. They hated and dreaded their annual trip with the Roman fleet to India, which to the old Phoenicians would have been a complete delight. There were now Red Sea ports, and at midsummer the fleet of 120 boats left for Ceylon or the Malabar coast of India, returning at midwinter with goods for which they had paid gold and silver. Italy produced nothing fine enough to attract the Indians.

Rome had good ships, but no port worthy the name. She depended on Alexandria to collect Egyptian and western Asian goods, and to supply fine manufactures of her own. Tyre and Athens were now feeble traders, and Delos was a slave market. The Gold Coast sent Rome its old products, and savage animals for the circuses. Spain still produced her metals, and in Toledo the famous steel blades were already being made. Rome neglected the Cornwall tin mines, partly because brass, a zinc and copper alloy, was edging out bronze. Southern Gaul and northern Italy supplied wool cloth and pottery, wine and olive oil, and cattle and hides they got from the primitive Germans at border fairs. The seas were now fairly free from pirates, and the *Pax Romana* protected the land routes, up to a point. Rome herself manufactured nothing, and exported little besides great quantities of gold and silver; she was almost wholly a receiving port, as the Empire itself was almost

THE ROMAN WORLD

wholly a receiving country living on the colonies.

Everything came into Rome, and she paid, not in goods made by busy workers, but in stolen gold. The people were given the official shows, and for the rest starved and stagnated. They were kept out of government, and had no useful place in the world, and so they were deeply unhappy; and population, which always increases when a country is confident, was actually decreasing. In the fourth century Rome finally adopted Christianity and built up the Catholic Church. But the early Church shared the general corruption, and could not provide the refuge the people needed. When the barbarians poured down over Italy, a good many slaves and common people went over to the enemy; perhaps they preferred them to the men of empire.

When the Roman Empire crashed in 476 the world fell apart. Rome had held it together only by force; and the Church was not yet strong enough to give the nations a common spiritual front. But the Church had made its peace with fairs. At first it persecuted them as nests of paganism, for though the people were nominally Christians they clung to the shrines and festivals of the gods. Under pretense of having a simple outing, they would go to the woods and under sacred trees sacrifice sheep and oxen to their beloved gods. The Church destroyed pagan idols and temples, and still the people flocked to the spots that had always been sacred to them.

The compromise which the Church gradually made was repeated in every country it entered: the people were allowed their shrines and festivals and even their holy days, but now they were all dedicated to the new Christian saints and martyrs. In general, the old fair sites remained fair sites with the blessing of the Church. By the time fairs were big and important again, the Church owned many of them, collected their revenues, and, when pressed for money, created more fairs.

The last fairs of the Empire belonged to the earliest and sturdiest type of all—border trade between the inhabitants and the invaders. The splendid power machine of the Caesars fell, and left the world almost as primitive, and far more wretched, than it found it. But the primitive fair survived, because the tribes of Europe had never learned other ways of trade; and Italy, Gaul, and Germany continued their border fairs. Otherwise, all was confusion; the pirates took back the seas, and the robbers the roads. Organized trade had collapsed, and that eternal lonely figure, the peddler, with his eternal comrade, the fun maker, ventured from town to town to scratch up a living. The *Pax Romana* was dead, and the peace of the fair sleeping.

In 629, in the midst of this confusion, King Dagobert of France in a solemn Latin edict created the Fair of St. Denis and bestowed its revenues on the Church. St. Denis is the patron saint of France, and in the Latin edict his name becomes Dionysus—that old Greek god of wine and merriment who presided over so many fairs in milder days. The pagan name of the Christian saint was only one of those accidents always happening to the Church, which did not cavil at names or at receiving its first great fair, which for well over a thousand years remained "the most royal fair of France." It was also the merriest and the most given over to wine.

4

VOYAGE TO CATHAY

WHEN he was seventeen, Marco Polo sailed from Venice with his father, Nicolo, and his uncle Maffeo, who were important merchants, bound for a land far in the East called Cathay. That was in 1271, and for twenty-four years nothing was heard from them, and they were given up as lost. Then one day three ragged tramps knocked at the Polo house, forced their way in, and told their

VOYAGE TO CATHAY

incredulous relatives that they were the lost Polos, and would like to give a banquet to celebrate their safe return.

At the banquet the travelers appeared in robes of crimson satin, which they soon changed for finer ones of damask, then for costly velvet, and finally for the usual Venetian costume, each time presenting their discarded finery to their guests. After the meal they sent away the servants, and, producing the old padded suits they had worn home, slit them open and showered on the table a dazzling heap of rubies, diamonds, sapphires, pearls, and emeralds. It looked like a treasure big enough to buy the whole noble city of Venice, and everybody admired the Polos' shrewdness in disguising themselves as beggars who would not interest the most enterprising thief.

The unsightly bundles they carried revealed more treasures. In Marco's, along with some silky yak's hair and Tibet musk, was a bequest to Europe—some worn notebooks that contained details of his travels through the realm of Kublai Khan and the countries of the East. This was a much greater treasure than the heap of jewels, for it gave Europe its first detailed knowledge

THE BOOK OF FAIRS

of the whole continent of Asia. Incredibly enough, Europe knew almost nothing of the countries that had sent it silk and spices for so long. The Arabs, Persians, and Syrians who handled the Eastern trade knew something of the Orient, but these people were no longer neighbors of the Great Sea; they were the infidel followers of Mohammed, the Saracens Europe was fighting in the Crusades. And none of them had notes to compare with Marco's.

Imagine what it would be to have the whole world dark except the one lighted strip taking in Europe, North Africa, and western Asia—a fifth of the globe. Marco enlarged this narrow world that Europe knew to cover more than half the northern hemisphere. If we lay the world out flat in a map fifteen inches across, Europe's bright strip covers three inches, and the dim section of Asia which Marco lighted up, four inches. Two centuries later Columbus, inspired by Marco's travels, and insisting that the world was round, sailed west instead of east to find Cathay, and covered two more inches on our map. The last six inches, which is the vast stretch of the Pacific, was added thirty years later in the heroic voyage of Magellan.

VOYAGE TO CATHAY

Three years after his return Marco was taken prisoner by Genoa during her trade war with Venice, and spent his time in jail expanding his notes into a long account of his travels. This astonishing and delightful book spread over Europe in Italian, French, and Latin versions written on parchment, and later in printed books. But for a long time people read it for entertainment rather than for the mine of information it contained, much of which they simply did not believe.

How, for instance, could the hard-headed merchants credit Marco's tales of Kinsai Fair, which ran in ten sections every third day, and attracted half a million customers? The Champagne fairs, running in one section, and with no such crowds, managed to clear the whole trade of Europe. And what about the five and a half tons of pepper that Marco insisted was sold in Kinsai every day? When he talked of the Great Khan receiving 100,000 pure white horses for his birthday, and watching his magicians make gold cups of wine float through the air, that was a tale told to amuse people. But when Marco talked about China's trade he had all the air of a careful merchant, checking Kinsai's sales against port receipts, and noting down exact figures. Five and a half tons of pepper a day meant that China used a hundred times as much as the whole of Christendom, and that was sheer nonsense.

Europe, with its small population, could not visualize the vast dimensions of China or its teeming cities. It knew so little of Japan, India, Java, Sumatra, and Ceylon, and Marco's account of these countries was so incredible, that he was nicknamed "Marco Millions" for his big talk, and died with the reputation of an inspired liar. By now we have discounted Marco's exaggerations, which were the fashion of the time, and checked enough of his facts to know that he was a shrewd and lively observer and a true merchant in that age which got most of its information from traders. To us the really astonishing thing about Marco's book is the incredulity with which Europe received it. We have seen the ancient caravans come back with goods from the Indies, and Roman matrons wearing silk spun in China. Why, if West traded with East for centuries on end, was the East unknown to Europe?

Europe's ignorance of Asia is one of the anomalies of trade history and requires some explanation. China was of course shut off from the rest of the world by the physical barriers of great mountains and deserts, but also by a dark wall of fear. And yet, having in 214 B.C. built the Great Wall as the symbol of this separation, China was at this same time, or shortly after, trading across the Pamir plateau with India, and sending her caravans across Tibet and western Turkestan, which by then were under her control. If we trace the story of silk, we will get some light on this trade.

Old records show that the cultivation of silkworms and the mulberry on which they feed was well established in China by 2640 B.C. For three thousand years China kept the secret of making silk to herself, but by 100 B.C. she was shipping it down to India by sea, and also sending it across the Pamirs by caravan, some of it bound for India, some for western Asia. The Arabs and Persians were active in the silk trade, of which Persian merchants for some time had the monopoly, establishing a colony at Ceylon, to which Chinese junks made regular trips, and to which, for a century or so, the Roman fleet made its excursions. During the first century of our era, China actually sent a trade embassy to the Persian Gulf, and after that had other direct contacts with her western neighbors, adopting the Indian Buddhism, allowing a few Arab and Persian traders to enter China itself, and giving asylum to members of the Nestorian Christian cult banished from Syria in the fifth century. These contacts did not affect Europe, more and more cut off from the Levant, and doing her small trade for eastern goods through Constantinople.

During the Dark Ages the secret of making silk began to leak out. India somehow learned the process; according to the legend, a Chinese princess coming down to marry an Indian brought mulberry seeds and silkworm eggs hidden in her elaborate headdress. Whether or not that is true, in 550 some Persian monks arrived in Constantinople with these same germs of the industry hidden in bamboo tubes, and taught the Greeks the stolen secrets of making silk. In the eleventh century the Arabs were the thieves, and smuggled the industry to Spain. By Marco's time Lucca in Italy was making the finest silk in Europe.

Even when the hordes of Jenghis Khan swept across Asia and camped in the plains of Hungary early in the thirteenth century, Europe learned little of these

VOYAGE TO CATHAY

Mongols and the country from which they had come. And though Europe very well knew that it could not have stopped the Golden Horde had it chosen to march straight across to the Atlantic, Europe was more concerned in preserving Constantinople from the Saracens. The new Mongol empire, which Jenghis' grandson Kublai inherited, stretched from the Pacific to the Dnieper River, and included Syria and Persia; but the empire of Islam worried Europe a great deal more.

The Crusades, which began with the effort to drive the Moslems out of the Holy Land, ended by building up trade and jarring feudal Europe from the narrow panicky life it had led since the downfall of Rome. The Crusaders were uncouth country folk who ate and wore what was produced on their manors. When they got to the Holy Land, the spirit of Tyre descended on them. Damasks and perfumes and carved ivory chessmen, the subtle eastern manners, and the whole atmosphere of luxury were new experiences. Feudal Europe saw itself as in a mirror, and realized that it was unwashed, rude, ignorant, and that it lived very badly indeed. Chinese sugar to replace the honey Europe had always used for sweetening was only one of the novelties the Holy Land had to offer. The first Crusaders came home with as much sugar and silk as they could carry, and a huge appetite for more.

Venice was now ready to seize this new luxury market. She had grown rich transporting and provisioning the troops; she had helped finance the early Crusades on terms that gave her in every captured town of Palestine and Syria a church, a counting house, and the right to trade without tolls. By shrewd twisting of the Crusade politics, Venice managed to supplant her rival Constantinople as Europe's trader; and wore the crown that had passed from Tyre to Athens to Carthage to Alexandria and then to Constantinople. She kept her rival Genoa down, and her galleys sped over the Great Sea picking up goods to send across the Alps to the fairs of Champagne.

In this pale golden city of the lagoons Marco Polo was born in 1254. His father and uncle had trading interests in the Crimea, and were seldom home; when Marco was six, they started off on one of these expeditions, and vanished. Marco spent his boyhood, we may be sure, hanging around the docks of Venice and asking sailors for news of the Polos. None of the Black

VOYAGE TO CATHAY

Sea traders knew what had happened to the elder Polos. Finally, when Marco was fifteen, they came home. Where had they been? At the court of Kublai Khan, no less. Nine years before they had made their way to Bokhara, and there had met envoys of the Khan, who were enchanted with the Venetian gentlemen, the first Europeans they had ever seen. They told the Polos that Kublai had now established his capital in Pekin in North China, and was conquering the Sung kingdom in South China. They begged the Polos to come back with them to the Khan, who had a great desire to meet Europeans.

It was as simple as that to get to Cathay, if you didn't mind the toils of travel. Kublai had been most kind, and asked all sorts of questions about Europe and its religion, and finally begged the Polos to go back as his ambassadors and request the Pope to send a hundred missionaries to convert the people of China.

The Church missed a great opportunity, for when the Polos started back with Marco two years later, it assigned only two Dominican friars to convert Kublai's vast realm—and they were so terrified at the journey ahead of them that they fled home. The three Polos

THE BOOK OF FAIRS

pushed on, taking one of the old silk roads across the Pamirs to Kashgar, across the Gobi to Tangut—three and a half years of dangers and hardships that would have downed anybody but a Polo. What they saw on this amazing journey is all set down in Marco's book. They finally reached Kublai's court, where they were welcomed like members of his family, and they stayed for eighteen years.

Marco quickly learned the languages of the country, and Kublai treated him like a godson, and relied on his judgment and his talent for meeting situations. The Great Khan was a conqueror living in a vast country of which he knew little; only two generations from Jenghis, a tribesman living in tents and drinking mare's milk. Jenghis, before he started west, had conquered Cathay in the north, but Kublai was still fighting the Sung kingdom in the south, and finally subdued it the year after the Polos arrived. South China, or Manzi, was the seat of the old civilization, and Kublai sent Marco on many missions of investigation into Manzi. On these trips Marco took notes of anything that might instruct the Khan, adding details for his amusement; so the book that grew out of these notes was

VOYAGE TO CATHAY

the report of a merchant ambassador to a half-barbarous conqueror about a country new to them both.

When he wrote his book in prison, Marco included descriptions of all the parts of China he visited under the protection of the Khan's golden tablet, which gave him wonderful opportunities for observation. He included also the account of the land journey across Asia and the voyage home, when he stopped at the East Indies and India. And he went into such rhapsodies about the splendors of the Khan's court that the modern mind almost bogs down under their weight. Probably Marco did not exaggerate much, for it takes a barbarian suddenly possessed of unlimited power and wealth to reach the limits of ostentation. Coleridge, reading Marco's book, dreamed that night his matchless poem, "In Xanadu did Kublai Khan a stately pleasure-dome decree," distilling this whole fabulous world into a few lines. Kublai's golden palaces and scented groves are best left to dreams; we are following Marco the merchant.

In Pekin he began to get an idea of China's industry, for the city was the center of two hundred busy towns making silk, and a thousand cartloads of raw silk came to Pekin every day to be spun and woven. As he went through the country, he found everywhere peace and plenty, for the country was vast in population, and everybody was working. He arrived at a time when China and the whole East were at a high pitch of production, and also of superb building. For the same spirit that caused the great cathedrals of Europe to rise was working in the East, and China, Indo-China, and the chief islands of the East Indies were producing marvels of architecture they have never since approached. Marco found a rapid system of posts, comfortable inns, rivers full of shipping, and everywhere the mulberry tree and the silk industry.

But the full force of Oriental trade only struck him when he first saw Kinsai, capital of Manzi. To the fairs of this town came China's products—tea, salt, sugar, ginger, camphor, porcelains, cloth of gold and gauzes of silk, lacquers, elaborately worked jewelry. Here was the spot where every province in China came to trade with other provinces and with India, Ceylon, Indo-China, Java, and Sumatra. Kinsai, City of Heaven, seat of the old Sung kings, had the greatest fair on earth, and it fascinated Marco more than any

MARCO POLO SEES THE LAND OF KUBLAI KHAN

spot he saw on his travels. He called it "beyond dispute the finest and noblest city in the world," and he was a Venetian.

Marco says that he visited Kinsai many times and wrote precise reports on it for the Khan, so he expects the world to believe what he says about it. But we do not have to rely upon Marco's descriptions alone, for there was a period after he left China when other observers were welcomed; and they too have left records of Kinsai which sustain Marco or go even farther. Here is Friar Odoric of the Italian town of Pordenone:

But if anyone should desire to tell all the vastness and great marvels of this city, a good quire of stationery would not hold the matter I trow. For 'tis the greatest and noblest city, and the finest for merchandise that the whole world containeth.

Another Italian, John De Marignolli, said:

Kinsai, the finest, the biggest, the richest, the most populous, and altogether the most marvellous city that exists now on the face of the earth, or mayhap that ever did exist.

Even when Marco says that Kinsai was enclosed by a wall a hundred miles in circumference—a claim not quite sustained by excavations in Hangchow, which now stands on the site—there is Wassaf the Persian to back him up. Wassaf said that Kinsai "stretched like Paradise through the breadth of Heaven," and that it was a three day journey across the city and its suburbs; but perhaps that was because of its attractions. And while we do not believe Marco's claim that 12,000 bridges crossed Kinsai's lagoons and canals, all travelers agree that there were hundreds of beautiful stone spans, ornamented with carvings and statues of the Sung kings. Medieval statistics aside, these bridges were arched high enough to admit masted ships under them, and so well graded that carts and carriages passed over them comfortably. They were the stations for the town police, who also acted as firemen. From the bridges the hours were announced, for the Chinese had water clocks.

Kublai kept a careful census, so we know that Kinsai had 1,600,000 "fires," or households. Since many families often lived under one roof, the city's population must have run into many millions. Such cities were undreamed of in Europe; even in 1600 the whole population of England was less than five millions. But this vast crowd of inhabitants, and the inns crowded with Chinese from the other provinces, and the suburbs for the colonies of established foreign merchants, were evidently kept in the most perfect order by systems of government and especially by the traditions of the people.

Kublai himself had nothing to do with the civic systems of Kinsai and the 1,200 other cities in the huge province of Manzi; these systems had grown up through centuries, creating such order and discipline that the Khan was content to leave them untouched. His only concern was to keep his new province under subjection, and to collect its revenues; and the garrisons he kept in each town took care of both. The Khan taxed all imports and certain goods like silk as much as ten per cent; and sugar, rice wine, Kinsai manufactures, and all domestic and export sales a third as much. He drew a small fortune every year from Kinsai's salt marshes alone.

So Marco's description of Kinsai gives us a picture of city life as it had existed under the Sung dynasty for the last three centuries. He details the admirable system for cutting down the fire hazard in this city of wooden houses and costly merchandise; its free hospitals; its strictness in providing every inhabitant with a job; its paved streets, its sanitary system furnished by a network of canals. Kinsai was evidently scrupulously clean. The Chinese bathed daily, and always washed before meals, and there were 3,000 luxurious public baths for the foreign merchants.

Kinsai was a manufacturing city of such dimensions that Wassaf the Persian said there were 32,000 dyers alone. The trades were organized into guilds; and, according to Marco, the twelve chief guilds each had a thousand workshops. But these shops were as a rule not large, for under the Chinese system the masters of the crafts had the factories near their own houses, and ran them as family concerns inherited from their fathers. Even if a master was too rich to work with his own hands, he was supposed by the firm tradition of the country to keep up his father's business. This system must have made conditions of work easier than in big factories, and certainly it kept the city attractive. For the Great Street which ran the entire length of Kinsai was lined with the fine houses of the guild masters, and these houses and the family workshops were set in large gardens.

From the Great Street, at intervals of four miles, opened the ten great squares where the fairs were held. The squares were uniformly built, and measured half a mile on each side. A wide shipping canal connected with the seaport twenty-five miles away ran parallel with the Great Street, and the canal side of the market squares was lined with stone warehouses to which the foreign merchants brought their wares. This ship canal, and Kinsai's network of smaller waterways, were all fed by the huge river that bounded one side of the city. On the other side was Western Lake, used for a pleasure resort. But let Marco tell of these great plazas:

"All the ten market places are encompassed by lofty houses, and below these are shops where all sorts of crafts are carried on, and all sorts of wares are on sale, including spices and jewels and pearls. . . . In each of the squares there are two great palaces facing one another, in which are established the officers appointed by the King to decide differences arising between merchants, or other inhabitants of the quarter. It is their duty likewise to see that the guards upon the several bridges in their respective vicinities are duly placed, and, in cases of neglect, to punish the offenders at their discretion."

This short description of the fair organization tallies with the rules laid down in the ancient Rites of Chow-li—the square surrounded by shops, in which the precious goods are sold, the officers who not only have authority to settle on the spot disputes between merchants but exercise a strict supervision over the whole district around the fair, and the police assigned to it, who are accountable to the fair guards rather than to their own chief of police. This is our first picture of a classic medieval fair, and though this one grew up completely independent of Europe, its general set-up is like those of Europe going on at the same time.

The fairs were held every third day, and Kinsai was furnished besides with many local daily markets. But the fairs sold fabulous quantities of freshly killed meat, vegetables and fruit, and fish brought from the sea and from the Western Lake. Marco describes the delicious pears weighing ten pounds, the yellow and white peaches, the imported wine and raisins. He almost wrings his hands over the bales of pepper from India, and the piles of fresh game and fish bought by these people who live so well (and not the rich alone) that they eat meat and fish at the same meal.

Kinsai was a legend in China for its luxurious habits. Almost everybody wore silk, which was of course abundant. "The houses of the citizens are well-built and richly adorned with carved work, and the delight they take in decoration, in painting, and in architecture, leads them to spend in this way sums of money that would astonish you." They lived "as nicely and delicately as if they were kings and queens. The wives indeed are most dainty and angelical creatures!"

Kinsai's recreations were perfectly adapted to people of many countries. The merchants and hospitable citizens could hire a luxurious carriage with silken curtains and cushions and roll over the smoothly paved streets to garden pavilions where they would sit for hours enjoying the freshness of the gardens and drinking "precious thunder tea" or, in hot weather, wine of snow bubbles and apricot blossoms, served in bowls of pure silver. Or they could enjoy a long evening on the Western Lake, floating in a gaily painted pleasure barge equipped to serve them meals on the water or on the shore in picnic fashion. The lake was gay with these bright barges, snatches of songs in Chinese, Persian, Arabic, and exchanges of nonsense as the barges passed each other and their passengers pelted one another with oranges and lemons. They could stop at one of the pavilions that dotted the lake and its islands; at the "Lake Prospect Chambers" or the "Eight Genii" or the "Pure Delight" there were dancing girls and singing girls and conjurors. Or one could merely float and enjoy the view:

"And truly a trip on this Lake is a much more charming recreation than can be enjoyed on land. For on the one side lies the city in its entire length, so that the spectators in the barges take in the whole prospect in its full beauty and grandeur, with its numberless palaces, temples, monasteries, and gardens, full of lofty trees, sloping to the shore."

This is an idyllic picture of a medieval Chinese city; so perfect that we begin to wonder if there could have been such a city at all. But Marco has something further to say about Kinsai that sets it apart from all other cities in China, and gives it reality:

"The natives of the city are men of peaceful character, both from education and from the example of their kings, whose disposition was the same. They know nothing of handling arms, and keep none in their houses. You hear of no feuds or noisy quarrels or dissensions of any kind among them. Both in their commercial dealings and in their manufactures they are thoroughly honest and truthful, and there is such a degree of good will and neighborly attachment among both men and women that you would take the people who live in the same street to be all one family.

"They also treat the foreigners who visit them for the sake of trade with great cordiality, and entertain them in the most winning manner, affording them every help, and advice on their business. But on the other hand they hate to see soldiers."

Marco visited many other great cities in China, but pays them no such tribute. Even in tranquil Manzi with its old culture, Kinsai was a city apart that lived under a perpetual truce. As Marco wrote, he was a prisoner in an ugly trade war, in a Europe perpetually upset with large and small broils between cities and nations. And yet in the midst of these anarchies there were islands of peace, the fair towns that banished arms and quarrels and unfair dealings. We have no idea how long Kinsai had been living under the special peace of the fair, but since its people had learned the habit of being honorable and gracious to strangers, and to their own neighbors, which is much more difficult, that peace must have been going on for a long time.

5

JEAN GOES TO CHAMPAGNE

AT about the time Marco Polo was checking the Kinsai pepper sales, a French leather merchant of Toulouse was on his way up to the May Fair in Champagne. We will call him Jean le Marchand (John the Merchant), a proud name, and one which sets the thirteenth century off from the long ages when the world dragged along without merchants or trade worth the name. We are apt to think this the greatest of all centuries because of its mighty cathedrals, its universities that met a sudden hunger for knowledge, and its Church, which at that time was strong and wise enough to lead the people forward. We think of this as the age of Dante and Roger Bacon and Thomas Aquinas, and Cimabue, who taught Italy how to paint.

But Jean le Marchand, a free merchant of the province of Languedoc, riding his horse up through cities glorious with their new cathedrals to a great fair where he would meet merchants from all over Europe, was perhaps the crowning triumph of the thirteenth century. Jean was an average man of forty, selling leather for a living—what is wonderful about that? The fact that he was free; that he belonged to a whole new class that was fighting its way to freedom and was eventually to rule society; and that he was a merchant. The mighty force that was pushing the arches of the Gothic cathedrals higher and ever higher was bursting the hard shell of the feudal world and creating cities, trade, and merchants, and these were creating the new middle class.

Jean's ancestors, not so far back, had been serfs liv-

JEAN GOES TO CHAMPAGNE

ing on a manor belonging to a feudal baron. His great-great-grandfather had been worth a third as much as a plow horse, and, like a horse, he could be sold. He could not move away, or even run away. If he married, or went to a fair, he had to have his baron's consent and pay him a fee. As the old troubadours said, if he had a fat goose or a bit of white flour in his bin, they went to the baron. When he died, his right hand was cut off and sent to the baron as a sign that a hand that had worked unceasingly for him was useless now. The troubadours, who said many biting things under the pretense of amusing people, put it this way: "God, when he created the world, made three kinds of people: nobles, clergy, and serfs. He gave the land to the nobles, the tithes and alms to the clergy, and condemned the serfs to work all their lives for the other two."

That had been the world a little while back—a world in which the nobles lived on the labor of their serfs and perpetually fought other nobles for more land and more serfs; a world in which the Church owned nearly half the land in Europe, and in which the king was an insecure overlord who dared not call his realm his own. A while back the peddler, who had no rights and no standing, had lodged outside the towns in places where roads and rivers met, and he was protected by the old gods of the crossways. And the first towns that grew up out of the devastation left by the barbarian invasions were on the old fair sites protected by the pagan gods.

Gradually the Church saw that the best way to bind the people together was to encourage trade and industry. It kept the industrial arts alive by its trade schools; it revived the old pilgrimage fairs and forgot their pagan origin; it began buying old fairs and creating new ones. Presently the barons realized that the Church was drawing enviable sums from its fairs, and began granting privileges to fairs in their domains. And finally the kings, especially Philip the Fair, now on the throne, began to think that fairs were a royal prerogative; and his meddling finally helped to ruin the great Champagne fairs. In general, this was an age when kings were drawing land and power from the barons; the Church was gathering up spiritual power and losing land; and trade, encouraged by king, Church, and barons, was building up cities and merchants who continually fought all three to win their place in the world.

JEAN GOES TO CHAMPAGNE

But the merchant had emerged from this struggle; and here was Jean le Marchand, a free man planning to marry his daughter Marie to the best possible husband and not somebody chosen by a baron, and taking his son Louis up to Champagne to learn to be a great merchant, like those supreme traders, the Lombards of central Italy, who came to Champagne to conduct the commercial transactions and the banking for Europe. Jean would sell his cartloads of leather for sound weighed money—another new accomplishment—and with it buy a dozen linen sheets from Rheims for Marie's wedding chest, and a length of Lucca silk to make the goodwife a gown. But beyond all this, he was a member of a class, belonging to a merchants' guild, which could fight for its rights; and beyond that again, he was protected by merchant law and by all the power of the Champagne Fair Guards, who could make the world of trade obey their decisions.

Champagne now meant not so much a province as a neutral center for the whole of Europe which was the tribunal of trade. The Counts of Champagne had built up the fairs in four towns—Troyes, Provins, Bar, and Lagny—all of them old fairs, but none outstanding except Troyes, which had started in the fifth century and been one of the favorites of that fancier of fairs, Charlemagne. The Counts had realized that Champagne was the geographical center of Europe's trade, near Germany, and also half way between the Flemish and the Italians, the two peoples most important in trade and industry. Their province was threaded by the great rivers of France; and soon they made it the hub of good roads radiating in all directions. With generous concessions in not taxing merchants too heavily, with courteous doles of part of the fair income to keep the Church satisfied, the Counts of Champagne soon had the world trading in the four towns.

Provins and Troyes were allotted two fairs each, and the smaller towns of Bar and Lagny one. Each ran two months under the same system and officers, who moved from town to town like the merchants. The year began at Lagny, then the Bar fair opened, and then, depending on when Easter fell, the May Fair of Provins (to which Jean le Marchand was bound), followed by the Warm Fair at Troyes, the Autumn Fair at Provins, and the Cold Fair at Troyes.

Louis and Jean were traveling with other merchants

JEAN GOES TO CHAMPAGNE

from the Toulouse Guild, and they were all armed, and headed by their consul, but had no particular escort. But the Lombards they met on the great Rhone-Saône valley route had men-at-arms and escorts furnished by the Champagne fair authorities, for they were carrying costly goods and a large amount of money. Some of this money would be used in fair transactions, some would be sent to supply the sixteen houses the Lombard bankers kept in Paris, but the bulk was a loan to King Edward of England or the Archbishop of Cologne or a Flemish town—one never knew what big business these men of Milan and Florence were in. But the world paid its debts and made new ones in Champagne because it was the one spot where complete safety and honesty prevailed.

That meant that all the routes to Champagne—the valley roads of the Rhine and Danube and the rivers of France and Flanders; the Alpine passes and the Italian roads that led to them; the lively traffic on the rivers themselves; and all the sea ways from Russia to Ireland to Cadiz and around the Mediterranean—all must be safeguarded. Against the pirates and robbers that infested seas and roads there worked a force truly marvelous—the peace of the fair. This peace was backed by international treaties, by kings and popes and barons, by the Fair Guards and the Counts of Champagne, by the cities and their leagues like the Hansa League of the Baltic—and behind them all by the common feeling that fair roads were sacred, and that whoever transgressed this sacred peace was committing sacrilege.

The peace of the fair had no boundaries. Like the Church, it stood above the nations. But the fair truce was older and far more effective than the Church's Truce of God which forbade fighting on certain days of the week. The fair truce forbade violence to merchants during the whole time they traveled to and from a fair, which might be months. It took five or six weeks for wagon convoys to come up from Lombardy to Champagne, though the fair couriers and the post riders made it in almost half the time. During all this journey, on certain roads, and in the daylight hours, the merchants were protected by Champagne—that is, if they sold their goods only at these fairs. If a band of robbers made a sudden foray on a lonely part of the road, who was responsible for the loss? The baron on whose land the robbery took place.

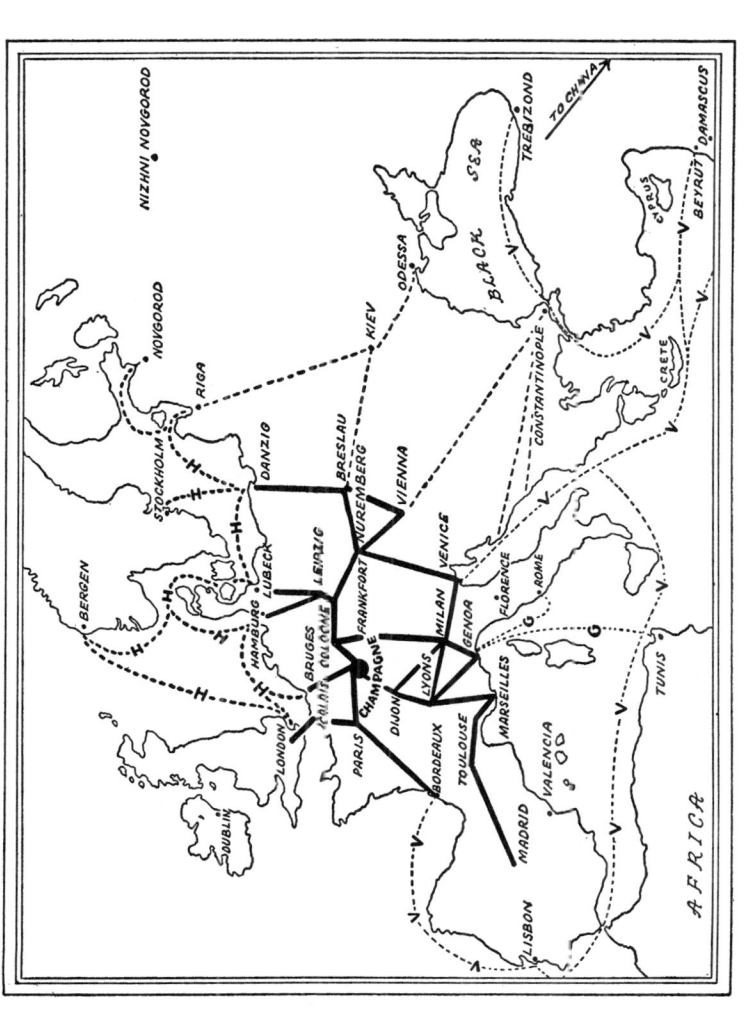

ROUTES TO CHAMPAGNE, 13TH CENTURY

HANSA LEAGUE --H--   GENOA --G--   VENICE --V--

JEAN GOES TO CHAMPAGNE

For instance, Thibault, Count of Champagne in the middle of the century, had demanded reparation from the Italian city of Padua for a theft committed near the city. Against whom? French merchants? Not at all, they were Italians, but they were on their way to Champagne, and the Count stood behind them and the safety of their goods. Other fair cities offered the same protection; Amiens had a law that said: "No one shall molest in their travels merchants coming to this city with their goods; and anybody daring to do so shall be seized by the commune and punished upon his body or his property as a violator of the commune." Champagne had abolished the iniquitous feudal right of the baron to inherit the goods of any traveler who "happened" to die crossing his land. It had fixed reasonable prices for food and lodging in the Champagne towns and on the roads.

The Toulouse merchants were friendly with the Lombards, and they all traveled along together, enjoying the wine of the country at the inns where they stopped at night, and amused by a French troubadour who had made the rounds of the Italian fairs, and by a little Gascon hunchback who obligingly ate fire or bits of glass, and swallowed swords. Since they were all bound for Champagne, the troubadour every evening sang part of the endless *Romance of Hervis,* that wound in and out of the fairs. One of the popular episodes was the story of lovely Beatrix, daughter of the King of Cyprus, who was stolen and taken up to Lagny Fair to be sold as a slave, but was of course rescued by Hervis in the nick of time. But the troubadour always got a shower of coins when he sang the "Merchants' Song" which began: "At Lagny, Bar, and Provins, there are merchants of wine, of wheat, of salt and herring, and of gold and silver and precious stones."

They left the Rhone Valley and followed the Saône River up to the city of Provins whose chateau towered over the sandy plain of Champagne. Provins was divided into the Low Town and the High Town built around the castle of the Counts of Champagne and the Church of St. Quiriace, patron of the city. Every big trading city in Europe had its own house in each of the four fair towns. In Provins it was considered the thing to be established in the High Town, which still had the air of a fortress. In fact, the Lombard financiers did their business in the castle courtyard, protected by its

JEAN GOES TO CHAMPAGNE

strong walls, and had their houses near by. Next to the money market in prestige came the cloth market, and many weaving towns had leased the big stone mansions of the High Town—Ypres and Cambrai, Flemish wool producers; Chalons and Troyes, which wove cottons and linens; and Lucca, the chief silk city of Italy. The Counts of Champagne cherished their fairs so much that they tried to keep the chief centers clustered around their castle, but for years the fair had been spilling down into the Low Town, and even then so many merchants flocked to Provins that a third city of tents was spread out on the plain.

The Toulouse house, which Jean proudly displayed to his son, was in the High Town on Saint Jean Street. It was called Forcadas, and as inn, warehouse, and place of business for the whole South of France, was one of the busiest centers of Provins. It was a three story stone mansion with vaulted ceilings supported by pillars, and underneath was a series of cellars for storing the leathers, wine, wax, honey, and red garance dye of the Midi. Besides Forcadas, the Toulouse merchants had another house on German Street in the Low Town, quarters in the central fair building, and shops and stalls on the fair ground.

Down in the Low Town certain sections were reserved for foreign merchants—here would be German Street, here Scotch Corner, and scattered through the town lodging houses and inns where a great deal of business was done over the red wine of Central France. Champagne was not yet making her famous wine, but the local province of Brie, which for three centuries was owned by counts in the family of the Counts of Champagne, had already perfected her exquisite cheese.

The fair ground was ancient, for it was on a site hallowed by Druid worship, on which the Church of Saint Jean now stood. Around it were shops and stalls arranged by strict divisions of merchandise. At the moment the Flemish merchants, who specialized in the cloth their cities wove from English wool, were getting ready to display their goods at the cloth sale which would open the fair. The Fair Guards had one office on the fair ground itself, and another in the central fair building in the Hôtel des Osches in the Low Town. Here the Chancellor kept the public scales and the great seal of Champagne for stamping documents which fair notaries drew up on the spot for any merchants who

JEAN GOES TO CHAMPAGNE

asked; the seal made contracts valid for thirty years. Certain privileged towns like Toulouse were allowed to display goods and make sales in this building.

Besides all the bustle of the merchants arriving by the network of roads and the two rivers, driving wagons and pack animals through the crowded streets, there was the life of the town itself. Provins, like the other towns of France, had drowsed through the Dark Ages, and now was humming like a hive. France was still far behind Flanders and Italy in industry, which was as new as the middle class, and cities, and the trade which was creating them. The Champagne fairs were not merely the most convenient meeting place for the traders of Europe, but were a tremendous stimulus to French industry, which was now producing goods to sell the foreigners. Provins had tanneries, flour mills, woolen looms, wine presses, rope factories, and a mint turning out coins which had a high rating in the welter of European currency.

But though there was bustle and confusion, the town preserved the special tranquillity that went along with the fair, and that banished even family feuds, which in that day might result in bloodshed. The old horror of polluting the sacred ground of the fair was still so strong that town peace and family peace were the rule in any European town holding fairs. The four Champagne towns were strictly policed, but what really kept them in order was the habit of many generations, and the overwhelming prestige of the Champagne system, which to the mind of the average citizen was as sacrosanct as the Church.

Jean le Marchand had brought his son into a spot which was neutral and international and also imbued with an inviolable authority, like the Vatican. If Jean could have looked into the future, or even if he had known enough about history and the world around him (thirteenth century people were vague in this respect) he could have described Champagne as a giant border fair which was gradually turning medieval merchants into modern business men by working out laws and principles which were becoming accepted all over Europe. By establishing a general merchant law, Champagne opened the way to free trade, which is possible only when everybody agrees to observe the same rules.

In Champagne there was already a medieval sort of free trade in the sense that merchants were regulated

JEAN GOES TO CHAMPAGNE

only by the international law instead of by local rules; duties and taxes were kept as low as possible; and there was for the first time a flexible money market. But kings and barons still had the last word about trade. For instance, the French king could command certain manufacturing cities to sell all their goods in Champagne, and certain other cities to trade only at the St. Denis Fair. There was an association of wool-weaving towns called the London Hansa, with headquarters in Bruges in Flanders. At first there were seventeen French and Flemish towns in the London Hansa, and finally there were sixty, but all of them were required to sell their wool cloth down to the last yard in the Champagne towns, and nowhere else. This royal supervision of trade turned out badly in the end; Philip the Fair, who acquired the province of Champagne on his marriage to Jeanne of Navarre, meddled so much with the fairs that he ruined them.

But we are looking at Provins in the 1280's, when the system worked out by the Counts of Champagne was still in force. At its head were the two Fair Guards, in some ways the most important men in France, and superior to the other officials of the province. They were appointed by the Counts and changed every few years; one was a merchant, the other a noble. They had charge of all six fairs, and went from town to town three days before the opening of each. On their shoulders rested the responsibility of the whole system; they judged and punished offenders, carried out ordinances, named sergeants and money changers, and made a general inspection of stalls and goods.

They were assisted by two chief clerks, by the Chancellor who stamped documents, and by an army of bailiffs, notaries, provosts, clerks, brokers, and inspectors. They had a staff of couriers who galloped down every road in Europe to deliver letters and messages. Less officially, the Guards were assisted by the heads of the merchants' guilds, who appointed representatives to sit with the Guards in settling legal disputes. The Italians had built up their city-states around the merchant guilds, and commercially they were so far ahead of the rest of Europe that their influence in Champagne was beyond reckoning.

The Fair Law (*jus nundinarum*), the first international merchant law, was a blend of the Roman code, the old trade customs of the Franks, and a general tradition of commercial practice which had been worked out around the Mediterranean. Rome had done badly with its fairs when it substituted state authority for fair authority, but Champagne, having to act as a neutral center, based its law on the peace of the fair. This made it possible for the Fair Guards to deal with offenders on the spot, and if they escaped before they were punished, to cross national boundaries to enforce their decrees. If a merchant fled Champagne without paying his debts, then the Fair Guards would compel his city to collect from him. If a city defied this order, it was forbidden to trade in Champagne until the matter was settled. The great cities of Lucca, Florence, and Cologne had all been suspended at various times, and their repentance was speedy.

Holding the same threat of expulsion over a French or foreign city, the Fair Guards could force local governments to redress wrongs committed against the humblest merchant. If a Norwegian or Polish trader had suffered some violation of the merchant law in his own country, he had only to appeal to Champagne to get speedy and effective justice. Here was the first international tribunal for merchants, and the one law and one authority for the trade of Europe. The fairs of Champagne, of Flanders, of Europe in general, were all asylums for merchants, who could not suffer arrest or seizure of goods for any crime committed elsewhere. As long as the fair peace lasted other laws were suspended.

Champagne kept down offenses against the peace of the fair—selling bad goods, cheating, failing to pay debts, and disturbing the peace—by careful inspection of goods and supervision of sales, by strict policing, and by setting aside the last month of the fair for the payment of debts, changing of money, and regulation of accounts. The whole financial side of business was still so new to everybody that it had to be conducted slowly and carefully.

Before the fair opened there was a week of unpacking and inspection of goods. The clerks with their true scales (our pound Troy comes from the Troyes Fair) met the barges on the rivers and the wagon convoys on the roads, and went into the merchants' houses to weigh, to measure, and to inspect goods for quality. By now all the merchants had assembled, and were making informal visits from house to house to examine goods and plan their purchases. And the retail shops of Pro-

JEAN GOES TO CHAMPAGNE

vins were working overtime, for when the fair opened all local trade was suspended.

We can imagine young Louis le Marchand waking up on May Day and staring at the fine pillars of Forcadas, all expectancy because this was the festival of the city's patron St. Quiriace, which would open the fair. He would hear the cry of the Hot Bath Man outside the window, and with his father go to have a bath and a shave. They would wear their best cloaks of Flemish wool with collars of mink.

They went to the high mass in the Church of St. Quiriace, and watched the splendid procession of the bishop attended by all his clergy. With merchants from the whole of Europe they knelt while the bishop gave them his benediction. And they listened to the oath of the Fair Guards to observe the customs of the fair, and to assist its merchants with every power in their command.

Now the Cloth Fair opened, and for the next twelve days nothing was sold but woven stuffs—the wool of the London Hansa, the silk of Lucca and the East, the gauze-like cottons of India, and the linen which was the glory of Rheims and the other Champagne towns.

Now that people had begun to wear underclothes and nightshirts, linen had taken a spurt. It was much cheaper than cotton, and the towns of northern France had so perfected their specialty that Rheims linen was as famous as Lucca silk.

Promptly on the twelfth day the sergeants rang bells all over town and cried, *"Hare, hare,"* a mysterious word which meant that the next division was about to begin, and the Cloth Fair had ended. The Furs and Leather division lasted for eight days. Leather was important because it was used not only for jerkins and shoes but for saddles, carriages, and upholstering furniture. Russia, Norway, Poland, and England, members of the great Hansa League that controlled Baltic commerce, sent unworked hides. The fine tanned and dyed leather came from Spain and from the South of France that had learned from Spain how to handle leather. The cordovans which everybody prized had originally been made in Cordova in Spain, but were now produced all over Jean le Marchand's section of France. Costly moroccos used for binding the vellum and parchment books that some people owned came from Spain and Portugal, and were made of fine goatskin. There was

JEAN GOES TO CHAMPAGNE

some competition in shoe and saddle leather from the Champagne tanneries, which were doing well with the sheepskins which were almost the only product of that sandy county. But Jean's cordovans never went begging, and the mountains of leather stored in Forcadas melted quickly.

The fur market going on at the same time in the houses and stalls of the Hansa League merchants was lively, too, for furs were cheaper than wool, and even poor people wore them and trimmed their clothes with them. Fur was also popular for bed covers, though it did attract the fleas. But any housewife worth her salt was supposed to spend part of each day killing fleas.

While the Cloth and Leather divisions were going on, there were separate fairs in other parts of town for the sale of goods bought by the pound, which included the important item of spices; for all sorts of manufactures like copper pots and furniture and shoes; for wheat, wine, and fresh food; and for metals of all sorts. There was a big livestock market, and a slave market that was getting smaller every year. During the earlier Crusades there had been a lively trade of European boys and girls to Saracens, and of Saracens to European masters. But the barons had discovered that slaves didn't work as hard as serfs who had a chance of earning their freedom by hard work and saving. So the slave trade was dying out.

The third chief division of the fair, the money market, now opened. Up in the castle courtyard in the High Town the Italian money changers got out their assortment of coins. And what an assortment! Taris, sequins, ducats, florins, pounds, maravedis, deniers, dinars, marabotins, coined by cities and dukes and kings —only a Florentine could keep it all straight. But certain coins were well made and fairly uniform in weight, and had the greatest vogue. These were the French *gros tournois,* which was accepted all over Europe, the English sterling, and the Florentine gold florin.

Patiently the Lombards weighed and changed money, which was a chore; and did the banking business for Europe, which made history. Nowadays most money operations are done with "paper," and this time-saving device started within the feudal walls of the Counts of Champagne. The bill of exchange or "fair letter" was our promissory note. It was a stamped document promising the payment of a certain sum to the bearer or his

JEAN GOES TO CHAMPAGNE

agent at a definite time, preferably at a reputable fair anywhere in Europe.

Another momentous improvement, which the Counts of Champagne had persuaded the Church to allow, was the essential business of borrowing and lending money. This had been a scabrous illicit operation condemned by the Church as "usury," carried on mainly by Jews who had been forced to charge scandalous interest rates to balance their risks. Now money lending was respectable in the extreme, interest ran from six to thirty per cent, and the Church itself was a chronic borrower at Champagne. The Archbishop of Cologne borrowed $200,000 (a fortune then) at Champagne; other prelates, and the Pope himself, were only too glad that usury was ended, so that the Florentines could tide them over difficulties. Edward of England did his borrowing in Champagne, and so did the city-states of Europe. The Lombards had eighty branch houses scattered over the Continent, and were spreading out into the first land and marine insurance, and into what we would call investment loans in commercial undertakings.

So Champagne was an international stock exchange in embryo, gradually prying business loose from Church superstitions and general distrust and confusion, and making it a free and flexible machine. The whole financial groundwork of trade was laid down here, experimentally and crudely enough, but on principles that are still at the heart of modern business.

The last two weeks of the fair wound up its internal affairs. Everybody paid his debts, and the fair notaries cast up the accounts from the beginning of sales. Meanwhile the merchants packed up their surplus goods to take to their houses in Troyes for the Warm Fair. Jean le Marchand was leaving early in order to take Louis up to the St. Denis Fair which ran from the eleventh to the twenty-fourth of June. The fair, held on the plain between the Cathedral of St. Denis and the heights of Paris, was a festival for the students of the University of Paris. They took part in the horseback procession across the plain, and paid their professors with gold pieces stuffed into lemon skins. The professors and the Rector of the University had other rewards; they did not share in the general carnival, but retired to the Abbey of St. Denis, which drew the revenue from the fair, and discreetly drank many a cup of wine in honor of St. Dionysus and his royal fete.

JEAN GOES TO CHAMPAGNE

Not that Louis had found Provins dull. On every street corner, in every tavern, were the troubadours and fun makers. The entertainers had a guild, like the merchants. They were prosperous nowadays, and went about in silk and fur, like the best. Some of the troubadours, who were poets making their own songs, and the minstrels who merely played and sang, and jongleurs who burlesqued the troubadours and minstrels, were so popular that lords and bishops would not sit down to dinner until they had had a song or two, accompanied by the viole and rebec. Music was everywhere, and so were entertainers: trainers with dogs and bears, exhibitors of freaks and of strange animals brought back by the Crusaders, Saracen dancing girls. There were acrobats and tumblers, and astrologers in long robes painted with the signs of the zodiac.

But the merchants loved best the puppet shows that acted out the romances they knew by heart. And there was a novelty, the Miracle plays acted by strolling players on a rude platform. They were something like the sacred plays acted in the churches by the monks, but these had been in Latin, and now the strolling players were presenting the holy stories in French, with broad splashes of farce. The scenarios had scope. One play began with the Creation, depicted Adam's Fall, and then the whole life of Christ, ending with the Ascent into Heaven.

Sometimes the whole town had a carnival, with everybody in masquerade. Lords would dress as swine-

herds, and swineherds would trick themselves out in ragged silks and velvets as cavaliers. There were pages and majordomos and queens with long robes and crowns, and merry monks and Crusaders and humble apprentices trying to look like guildsmen. The streets were thronged with the crowds that danced and joked and sang with the troubadours. At the end of the revelry the armed sergeants of the fair, as on every evening, marched through the streets with flaring torches, followed by a band of fiddlers. Louis and Jean would climb the hill to Forcadas. Tomorrow they would go to Paris, and then come back to Champagne

JEAN GOES TO CHAMPAGNE

for the Warm Fair of Troyes, and by mid-September be in Forcadas again, watching every evening the streets flare with light as the sergeants passed, and then darken so that the castle walls were sharp against the night. For them, and for all the merchants of Europe, those walls enclosed a world secure, ordered, and perpetually at peace.

6

NEW GOODS AND NEW PLACES

EUROPE, in its swift passage from feudalism to modernity, was like a rocket that flies into the air and explodes in a shower of red and blue stars, then rushes higher and bursts into an even more dazzling shower. Some tremendous energy stored up in those nondescript ages when nothing seemed to happen was released in this rocket flight.

The thirteenth century was one such explosion, and

the fifteenth another. Between them there was a grim pause while the Hundred Years' War, the peasants' revolts, and the Black Death killed millions of people. Then, as if these dreadful things had not occurred, the glories of the Renaissance were created in the cities of Europe. The cities themselves were the highest work of the age—Florence, Venice, Lyons, Paris, Bruges, Antwerp, Lubeck, Cologne, Nuremberg—a galaxy of cities rich and beautiful, full of people painting and carving, building exquisite town halls and churches, weaving tapestries and velvets and gauzes, contriving mechanical toys and intricate locks and keys, casting bells, printing books—people enchantingly dressed, and robustly enjoying life.

This was the great age of painting, and the artists found inexhaustible material in the life of the towns. For the most part, they were independent little city-states like Athens. There is probably no better system for developing art and social life than the small world of the city-state; and none better for building up the sort of trade that has movement and color. The fairs of this period, modeled on those of Champagne, were as unlike them as a gusty *kermesse* scene by Peter Breughel is unlike an illumination on parchment. This is the age of the first printed books, but the art galleries tell a much fuller story of how people lived in the Renaissance.

On canvas, the age was joyous; on paper, complicated and full of dangers. By 1500 the foundations of modern Europe were laid down; and a mass of problems not yet solved was bequeathed to the future. Jean le Marchand, exulting in the creation of cities, trade, and the new middle class, gives way to his German brother Johann der Kaufmann, who is also proud of being a merchant, but has already run into difficulties. For population was increasing at a tremendous rate, industry was growing by its own laws, big ships navigating by the marine compass were exploring the globe; in short, progress was working at top speed, and progress always complicates things.

The Church was no longer the one strong power leading the people, and was being bitterly attacked by reformers like John Huss. The kings had won their fight with the barons, and now were fighting each other for power, as the feudal lords had fought each other. Wars and conquests were now on a large scale

NEW GOODS AND NEW PLACES

and affected the lives of more and more people. The kings devotedly built up international trade; they made fine roads and waterways, protected their merchant marines with treaties, and created fair after fair.

But one royal marriage could now change the fortunes of a whole country of fairs. Philip the Fair married the commerce of Champagne when he wed Jeanne of Navarre; but the Hapsburg Maximilian I married all the fairs of Burgundy and the Netherlands when he took young Marie of Burgundy for his first wife. It happened that Maximilian was a great fancier of fairs, but these shifts of whole civilizations from their familiar ways to an alien rule almost never produce anything but trouble.

The monarchs built up the trade of each country around themselves, and that meant that the cities were losing a certain power. Everything was on a national scale now, which was partly good and partly bad. The merchants, feeling this pressure, banded themselves into powerful associations, something like modern Chambers of Commerce. In England there were the Merchants of the Staple, who controlled the wool trade with Flanders, and the Merchant Adventurers, who thought that England should spin and weave her own wool. Paris had several federations of merchants, and Florence its Major Arts League.

Then there was the Hansa League of the Baltic and North Seas, which was now two hundred years old, and had a hundred trading cities as its members. The League controlled all the sea trade of northern Europe; it was a rather ruthless commercial state that made its own laws and treaties and protected its fleet from pirates with its own warships. From the fairs of Novgorod in Russia to the ports of the Netherlands, the League had a chain of fortified trading posts guarding its stores of salt fish, lumber, tallow, skins, furs, and metals.

These merchant federations had great power, and so did certain rich families like the Medicis of Florence and the Fuggers of Germany. For capitalism had already begun; and the new middle class was split into three parts, with men of great wealth at the top. The men in the middle—average merchants and masters of the crafts—were still fairly independent, but the workers at the bottom were being pushed down into something like the serfdom they hoped they had left

NEW GOODS AND NEW PLACES

behind. Also, the first factories were growing up. We would laugh at them now, but there were little factories with blast furnaces and machinery.

With such changes in society, fairs too changed in this century—in their goods, their location, and their methods of trade. Because of the Hundred Years' War, France is not in the fair picture of the fifteenth century, though her fairs, and those of Italy, were still important. But Champagne was no longer the meeting ground for the Italians and Flemish. The Venetians early in the fourteenth century began to send their galleys up to Flanders, and traded with France through the more convenient fairs in the south. In that century Lyons had the greatest fairs in Christendom, and Geneva was also a favorite place for foreign merchants. But Champagne lost the favor of the French kings, and her crown passed to Flanders.

Even in the days of Jean le Marchand, the Netherlands (later divided into Belgium and Holland), had international marts. There was a circle of Flemish towns—Thorout, Lille, Ypres, Messines, Bruges, and others—that had a month-long fair apiece and so kept a perpetual market going. These fairs, and the whole prosperity of Flanders, then the richest country in Europe, were based on the cloth industry that kept every Flemish town busy until the English discovered that they could weave their own wool.

The Flemish used to say, "We bought the skin from the English for a penny, and sold them back the tail for a pound." It was true; the English braved the pirates to bring their fleeces to the Flemish fairs, where they paid high prices for the cloth made of last year's fleeces. Finally, led by the Merchant Adventurers, England started her own looms and killed the chief industry of Flanders. This loss might have ruined the country except that it began to weave linen and Spanish wool, and did so well as Europe's chief merchant that it got along without a base industry.

Until the middle of the fifteenth century Bruges was the world's fair. She was head of the London Hansa that controlled the cloth industry, the funnel through which the Hansa League poured its Baltic goods, and the home of many industries besides weaving. She was the greatest money market in Europe, and the House of Medici had one of its chief branches there. Like Tyre, Venice, and Kinsai, Bruges was threaded by

NEW GOODS AND NEW PLACES

canals, and like them, she was exquisitely beautiful. A hundred ships stood in her harbor, and the town was radiant with luxury. When Philip the Fair brought his queen up to Bruges she looked at the richly dressed women everywhere and exclaimed, "I thought I was the only queen here, and now I see six hundred!"

Bruges had a Cold Fair and a two months' Easter Fair, which began with the Feast of the Holy Blood on May second, when every bell in town rang as the sacred relic was exposed. Bruges had a genius for pageantry; she hung her streets with cloth of gold and tapestries and her flags, which bore a black lion on a gold ground. The procession in this May festival had all the pomp and gusto of the days of chivalry; the cavaliers on horses caparisoned in rich cloths, the clergy and magistrates almost as splendid, the artisans and apprentices, the merchants' guilds, troops of archers, musicians blowing silver trumpets—all ending in a fine show of jousting and feats of chivalry and the annual archers' tournament.

At her fairs Bruges offered the world the new goods it was learning to enjoy. There were oranges, aloes, raisins, and olives from Spain, and pet monkeys and parrots the Spanish brought up from Africa. There were carpets from Persia and from the new factories in Brussels and other Flemish towns; and the first lace and tapestries from northern France. Italy sent wonderful works of art and craft; brocades and Genoese cut velvet and gilded Venetian leather. And from Germany came a whole assortment of novelties—keys and locks both intricate and beautiful, Nuremberg toys, bells, iron wire and nails, edged tools, carved furniture, inlaid armor, and pottery and glass almost equal to Italy's. There were novelties in cloth: the sturdy fustian, hollands and cambrics; and England's first experiments in friezes, kerseys, and worsteds.

But luxurious Bruges with her pageants, her skillful artisans, her harbor full of caravels from Spain and Italy, whose merchants found here in the north the charm of Cordova or Florence, by the middle of the century was called the Dead City, and 5,000 houses of foreign merchants stood empty. Bruges was killed by complications of every sort: her harbor silted up; she resisted the marriage of Marie of Burgundy to Maximilian and so was slighted by her new master; the English defected and began to sell their wools through their

NEW GOODS AND NEW PLACES

staple port Calais and the Antwerp fairs. But what really killed Bruges was her failure to march with the changes in trade.

There was a good deal of money in circulation now, and a vast population to serve. Trade had to break away from the narrow system that had been perfect for the Champagne fairs, which Bruges faithfully followed. In Champagne or Bruges the merchant himself brought his goods to the fair, and exchanged them for new goods which he took home. This classic sort of fair lingered on in Europe for another four centuries; its last survival was the Nizhni Novgorod Fair. But trade in general needed short cuts; and these it found in Antwerp.

One of the amusing facts in the history of fairs is that the first international stock exchange was born in a graveyard. In the cemetery of St. Marie in Antwerp, the merchants met and ordered goods of each other. This is the beginning of the system of *indirect* selling; the merchants did their business by ordering, instead of exchanging actual goods. That is, they began to buy and sell without having the actual goods under their noses; though the old direct trade still went on, and

THE BOOK OF FAIRS

Antwerp was crammed with foreign merchandise. But modern ways of trade began in the Antwerp graveyard, for reasons we sketched in the first chapter.

As we have seen, the ancient fairs of Egypt, Greece, and the British Isles were connected with worship of the dead and festivals in their honor. In the Netherlands and the British Isles this old pattern is constantly breaking through the thin top layer of civilization. The Church in these countries was forever forbidding the people to trade and dance in the churches and cemeteries, which merely proves how common these habits were. The famous Flemish kermesses (from the German *Kirchmessen,* or church fairs) romped in and out of churches and over gravestones. The fifteenth century Lille fairs were held in the cemetery of St. Etienne Church. In Antwerp there was an annual kermesse in the Church of St. George until it was destroyed in the French Revolution, and then the kermesse was held in the burying ground.

And so trade, plunging into modern ways, preserved the background of antiquity until in 1460 Antwerp built the first international Bourse or Exchange, and called the merchants from the cemetery of St. Marie.

NEW GOODS AND NEW PLACES

Antwerp was already taking advantage of the fall of Constantinople a few years before, and was stealing the spice trade from Venice, which began to go down. Full of the new liberal spirit of trade, Antwerp abolished old restrictions and taxes and left the merchants free to use their own methods. Loans were fixed at low rates; merchants were allowed to deal through agents instead of traveling to Antwerp themselves; and late in the century the foreign trading guilds moved over from Bruges, and a thousand foreign merchants were stationed in the city. In her fine port on the Scheldt two thousand ships stood at anchor, and an equal number of cartloads of goods came every day over the roads.

The Antwerp fairs were in the late spring at Pentecost and in August at the Feast of St. Remy, each lasting six weeks. The whole world was there, protected by sound treaties between Antwerp and the cities, and by the Church's safe conduct which allowed even merchants banned from the kingdom to come and trade. The volume of commerce at these fairs was much larger than in Champagne, and flowed with fewer restrictions. Antwerp, as the Venetian ambassadors admitted, did more business in two weeks than Venice did in a year. The ambassadors were impressed with the fine houses and luxury of the Flemish, with their business ability, which even the women shared, and with the gift for music which was apparently universal. The Venetians, who came from an older and suaver level of culture, hinted that the people of Antwerp were the least bit overdressed and careless in their manners, and that they had no notion of fine cooking. Still, they were friendly people with gusto, and even if they all loved money too much, they were clever enough to get it.

Antwerp doubled her population in a century and became one of the greatest trade marts of history, but there was one new product developed by Germany which now began to draw traders to the Leipzig fairs. That new product, which was to bring society so much good and harm, was the printed book.

Two things were needed for printing on a large scale—the idea of using carved movable blocks of wood each bearing a letter, and paper—and both came from China. Some people claim that Marco Polo brought back Chinese block books and taught Europe how to

NEW GOODS AND NEW PLACES

print. There seems to be no ground whatever for that tale. But some traveler who followed Marco Polo to China must have brought back books, for about this time there was a kind of printing or stenciling done near Venice that was strikingly like the Chinese. From then on, a patient army of unknown men experimented with the art of printing. We know that there was printing from movable blocks in Haarlem, Holland, in the first half of the fifteenth century, and this printing may have been done by one Junius Coster. But the first printer we are sure about was the German Johann Gutenberg, who started a shop in Mayence in 1438.

As for paper, which China had long used for books and money, that was brought west by the Arabs, to whom Europe was also indebted for sugar. In 751 the Chinese besieged Samarkand, which was held by Arab Moslems. The Arabs drove the Chinese back, and captured among others some skilled Chinese paper makers. At once the Arabs began writing their books on paper instead of the expensive parchment, but Europe at large paid little attention to this new material. Finally the Germans began to manufacture paper in the fourteenth century, turning out a product both good and cheap.

From then on everything worked together, and from the moment Gutenberg started his press, printing became a lively industry. William Caxton in England and Aldus in Venice followed on Gutenberg's heels, and soon the world was owning books and learning to read. The busy presses turned out the Bible, the writings of the Church Fathers, the works of Dante and Petrarch, of Bacon and Chaucer, but also the romances the people knew by heart, the tales of Parsifal, Eulenspiegel, Tristan, and William of Orange.

Germany, the last great country of Europe to become civilized, became the home of the book fair. It was a long cry from her pagan fairs, her slave marts where only a few centuries before war captives had been sold for a song, and other markets where wives had been sold for what they were worth as farm animals. But German trade and industry had developed very quickly. By now the league of sixty Rhine cities had a trading fleet of 600 boats, and on the Danube another fleet traded with Italy and the Levant. Germany was working her mines and turning their metals

NEW GOODS AND NEW PLACES

into finished goods.

The delightful town of Nuremberg produced the most masterly metal work, and there was often a whimsical turn in her wares, and a mechanical ingenuity matched nowhere else. The whole town was a toy factory, and soon these toys learned to dance and sing. The Nuremberg clocks that decorated town halls all over Europe not only kept perfect time, but put on puppet shows every hour. These faithful clocks with their bewitching little figures that march out on the hour for their performance are still amusing Europe.

The chief German fairs had started in the tenth century in Cologne and Mayence on the Rhine and nearby Frankfort on the Main. When printing began, these fairs, especially Frankfort, specialized in the book trade. Over in Saxony was Leipzig, with many printing shops and a new university which was becoming an important seat of learning. A lively fight to capture the book trade began between the Rhineland cities and Leipzig, whose Easter and Michaelmas fairs were already big markets for furs and other Baltic goods. When the Bishop of Mayence began to censor books and the Rhineland trade fell off, Leipzig seized her advantage and became Europe's book fair. Maximilian gave her a third fair at New Year's and a number of special privileges.

Leipzig was in a fine position for trade, especially with the newer countries to the south and east. Five great roads led out to every country of Europe, and on these roads, for eighteen days before and after fairs, merchants were protected by the Emperor's safe conduct and by the Cross Watch, a special guard named after the cross that was still the protector of traders. The old rule of fair sanctuary held; there were no arrests or seizures of goods during the truce. The Pope in an edict put the Leipzig fairs under the protection of God and of the apostles Peter and Paul.

Besides books and furs, Leipzig had a lively cloth trade centering in the huge Cloth House, and sold Hungarian leather, glass from her own province of Saxony, Austrian plated goods, and the Baltic goods of the Hansa League. She housed her foreign merchants in new buildings constructed around the marketplace where the fairs were held, and regaled them in her taverns with beer and music. Everybody seemed to

NEW GOODS AND NEW PLACES

sing and play in Germany as in Flanders; there were lutes, violins, harps, zithers, trumpets, portable organs, and clavichords, to say nothing of musical bells.

Most of the fair amusements had been developed along the Rhine and in Nuremberg, and now all the entertainers trooped to Leipzig. The Germans were thunderstruck by the first elephants exhibited at the fairs, but they became sophisticated in the arts of tight rope dancing and acrobatics, and were already sending performers over to the English Bartholomew Fair, and on general tours of Europe. At Leipzig there were the perennial trained animals and human monstrosities and fire-eaters, but also specialties like the automatons contrived by Nuremberg. There was the Priest from Littau whose mechanical dragon advised merchants on matters of trade or romance, and the first calculating horses who could change any piece of money into the proper coins.

And by now there were plays much more elaborate than the Miracle plays of Champagne. All over Europe the fair was developing amusement lines that were later to be divided into music-hall entertainments, circuses, and the stage. The theatre was born in the church and developed by the fair, especially in England. The priests in Germany were still performing the Passion Play and other Mysteries, but the Church had begun to frown on this, and meanwhile companies of strolling players set up their stages at fairs and performed not only Bible stories (mixed with burlesque and humor of the lustiest sort) but also the romances of Jason, Parsifal, and all the others the people were now reading in their new books.

The Leipzig fairs followed the religious festivals, which in Germany were celebrated with wild carnivals which had not lost the old pagan spirit or some of its rituals. Housewives still smoked evil spirits out of the house at Epiphany; sweethearts still jumped through the fires of St. John's Eve (Midsummer Day). On Shrove Tuesday all the towns put on masquerade costumes and sang and danced in the streets, and begged from house to house for honey cakes; Easter and New Year's were riotous carnivals.

And while the people danced, Columbus studied the book of Marco Polo and the voyages of Leif Ericsson to a country called Vinland, and presently persuaded Ferdinand and Isabella to send him on his voyage west.

NEW GOODS AND NEW PLACES

Five years later Vasco da Gama rounded the Cape of Good Hope and realized the old Phoenician dream of sailing around Africa to reach Cinnamon Isle. And not long after that Magellan's ships—or rather the *Vit-*

toria, the only one to survive—went clean around the world.

Now the pivots of world trade shifted, and Spain and Portugal in the south and England and Holland in the north became great shipping powers. From now on the story of fairs is laid not so much along land routes as the lanes of the sea. Just as ideas had filtered slowly and often incorrectly from person to person before the invention of printing, so goods had filtered slowly and often with damage and loss from one caravan to the next. We could represent the early history of trade and ideas alike by broken winding lines, and

THE BOOK OF FAIRS

the history that now begins by unbroken lines that run straight as the Roman roads. Immense time and labor began to be saved, and this surplus energy could now be used in colonizing America and building the modern world.

7

ENGLISH VARIETY

THERE are corners in the British Isles where fairs are still held in churchyards, and where the people believe fairies come to them. Something in England preserves old tracks in the minds of its people and in its very soil. You can see today the verdant circles of the Fairy Rings, and the long green trackways that four thousand years ago were the roads of pilgrims crossing England to Stonehenge and Avebury. It is wonderful to see the sun rise on Midsummer Day and strike the altar stone in the precise center of Stonehenge, but somehow more wonderful to see in the soft earth the ancient stamp of the pilgrimage roads. The greatest of these roads come together at Avebury Hill, where in the days of Babylonia and Cnossos the pilgrims gathered for their festival fairs.

Sun worship, moon worship, and sacred stones, trees, and wells, all come into Britain's fair story along with the worship of the dead that is bound up in the ancient Irish fairs. Most of them were held at the burial places of kings and queens; the old word *oanach* meant both cemetery and fair, for, like the prehistoric Greeks, the Irish honored their illustrious dead with games and jubilees. The Irish fairs were the centers of political and religious life, of law giving and judgment; every feis or assembly of the kings of Ireland and the part of Scotland under Irish sway, beginning with the great Feis of Tara, either grew out of an old fair or created one to go along with it. In this turbulent land where wars and feuds were a sacred obligation, the peace of the fair was so stringent that its violator was punished with death, even if he was of royal blood.

ENGLISH VARIETY

Tara Fair was held at the burial place of Queen Tea, Emain Macha Fair at the barrow of that Ulster queen, Tailte at the mound of still a third queen, Tailte, the foster mother of Lug, who was both a sun god and the patron of fairs. Tailte Fair, which lived well over two thousand years, lasted from mid-July to mid-August, and was an early harvest festival in which first fruits were sacrificed to the spirit of the dead queen, who was further honored by funeral games. Each chieftain brought his best athletes—runners, jumpers, spear throwers, horsemen—and also his harpers and poets and story tellers, who competed like the athletes for prizes of gold rings and jeweled ornaments. Multitudes of people from Ireland and Scotland came to the Tailteann Games; the last year they were held, in 1169, the line of chariots and horsemen on the road was six miles long. The fair itself lasted until 1806, and not long ago the Irish revived the Tailteann Games, as the Olympics were revived.

Carman Fair, celebrated "without breach of law, without crime, without a deed of violence, without dishonor," was held at the cemetery of ancient kings every third year in August. This rich fair is described in a long poem, which enumerates the things forbidden: to sue, to levy, to disown debts, to arrest or distrain anybody on the sacred ground of the fair. All personal jewelry and ornaments which had been pawned, or impounded for debts overdue, had to be released to the owners for the period of the festival. It was considered a disgrace for anybody to appear at these assemblies without his richest clothes and jewels. And, as in all Irish fairs, the history of Eire was sung by the poets, so that the people, hearing these sagas year after year, would remember their wars, cattle raids, romances, the genealogies of their kings, and the laws and precepts of their wise men.

Uisneach Fair in County Meath was a May Day festival for the sun god Bel, worshiped also in Scotland and Wales. In every district two "Beltane fires" were lighted, and a pair of each kind of cattle in the neighborhood was driven between them to preserve the herds from disease in the coming year. There are people alive today who have seen these Beltane rites, and the fair lasted till recently under its old name which means "Bel's Fire."

These fairs and all the others cleared the trade of

Ireland and part of Scotland in their markets for food, livestock, and luxuries. But romance was for sale, too; Tailte Fair especially was a marriage mart, where thousands of boys and girls were brought by their parents and betrothed, after the dowries had been arranged. This was the survival of an ancient custom, which lingered a long time in the British Isles and Gaul —the sale of wives for the term of one year. The early Irish law provided that a woman bringing no dowry to her husband could be sold to balance the score. The spot at Tailte Fair where the wives-for-sale sat and sewed while they waited for a new master is still called "Marriage Hollow."

The early fairs of Ireland and Scotland were almost the only occasions for peaceful contact between warring clans. The pattern of the Scottish fairs is so distinct and so perfect that it explains some of the mystery of the beginning of fairs all over the world. Here we can almost see them growing out of the ground. And here we see the northman of the sagas working out the peace of the fair amid the clash of arms.

The Picts and Scots and the island people from Orkney and Shetland had border fairs at fords, crossroads, the mouths of rivers, and at the holy wells. These spots were marked with a tall stone pillar on which the traders placed their hands and vowed to keep the truce. In the old harsh and superb law the people were commanded to keep the peace on pain of being outlawed. That was a death sentence, for nobody would feed or shelter an outlaw, but it carried a punishment far more grave, the wrath of the gods against the desecrator of peace.

As towns grew up at these trading spots, the pillar remained the center of tribal life and the symbol of the strict truce that protected the region around it. From the pillar the laws were given out, and around it trading was done. Any outrage or bloodshed in this area was sacrilege; if murder occurred, then the fair site was polluted and had to be abandoned. It became necessary to mark the limits of the fair peace, and so the custom grew up of "riding the marches." The Scottish *march*, and the German *mark*, mean border, and seem to be connected with the word *market*. The march riders before each fair set out from the trading pillar, taking along small boys who when they grew up would have to remember the limits of their town. These limits were marked with a big tree or a march stone, and at these spots the boys were dumped into ponds, or had their heads bumped on the march stones, to make them remember the place. The boys of early New England, by the way, were taken on expeditions of this sort.

Christianity only changed the externals of the old system. Sometimes the trading pillar remained, with a rude cross cut into it, sometimes a new column bearing a cross at the top was raised. The market cross continued to be the center of community life; laws were still given from its steps, and trade still clustered at its base. The people continued to hold their fairs at the holy wells and on certain days to dress the wells with flowers, so the Church built chapels and shrines in these spots, and dedicated many pagan fair days to Christian saints and martyrs.

In England, too, the old pagan habits died very slowly. Tan Hill Fair is still held near England's first sanctuary, Avebury Hill in Wiltshire, where the ancient trackways meet. Tan Hill was evidently the burial ground of Avebury, for it has five round barrows like the burial mounds of the American Indians.

THE BOOK OF FAIRS

All through the South of England there are still fairs near barrows, and these fairs follow the four seasons as in the days of sun worship. Maypole and Christmas dancing in the churches, fairs stubbornly held in the churchyards in the teeth of repeated Church laws; fair trading inside churches and cathedrals—these customs lingered here and there until our own times, though they originated in worship of the dead. As for moon worship, this seems to survive in the all-night "Sleepy Markets" still held in certain districts, and more remotely, in the English wakes. These were not wakes in the usual sense, but all-night vigils held in the church on the anniversary of its dedication or on its saint's day. The next day was a holiday, and a fair was held in the churchyard. Most of the English fairs were held at these wakes, so that each district had its annual festival and market. By the seventeenth century the list of fixed fairs ran into thousands, and no peddler or strolling fiddler could be without his "Book of Fairs" that told him where to go next.

The English variations on the peace of the fair are amusing. As in France, the King's glove was the symbol of his "firm peace" which he granted each fair in its charter, and we encounter this glove in many forms. In one Somerset town, the crier carried a huge gilded glove on a pole, and went through the streets shouting, "Oyez, oyez, oyez, the Fair's begun, the glove is up. No man can be arrested till the glove is taken down." Immunity from arrest was the general rule, as was the oath which each man took as he entered the fair gates, and which was oddly phrased: he promised not to lie, steal, or cheat, until he came out. In case he forgot, there were the stocks and whipping post on the fair ground, to which the Pie Powder Court could sentence him. This odd name is simply mispronounced French. Merchants were called "Dusty Foot" (*Pied Poudreux*), so the fair court became the Court of Dusty Feet.

A fair that combines an assortment of English traditions is St. Giles Fair near Winchester. To begin with, St. Giles Hill has a long barrow. When fairs first started on this hill only its worn old turf knows; William the Conqueror found it the center of the wool trade when he entered England, and granted it his charter. For sixteen days all the shops in Winchester and near-by Southampton were closed for the fair, and during it there was no authority for the whole district but the fair officers. On St. Giles Eve the mayor and bailiffs of Winchester went out of office and surrendered the keys of the city to the bishop and his officers of the fair. St. Giles drew traders from France, Flanders, and all England, until the wool trade moved to the east coast; then it became a local fair which still exists.

By the seventeenth century Stourbridge Fair near Cambridge became England's chief place of exchange, and by then England's trade was heavy. She had lagged far behind France and Flanders in industry, and behind Holland in shipping, and now was making up for lost time. Roused by the Merchant Adventurers, she was weaving her own wool at last, and had started the linen industry in Ireland. She was fighting the Barbary pirates who chased English ships up into their own Channel, and was killing Holland's magnificent sea trade with a ten years' war. She was sending her ships to India and the East Indies, and to her new colonies in America and the West Indies, and bringing back wealth and new goods that changed the habits of the nation.

Till well into the seventeenth century, Europe some-

"OYEZ! OYEZ! THE GLOVE IS UP!"

how existed without coffee, tea, or tobacco. Our own social life is so firmly organized around these blessings that it is difficult to picture our ancestors, hardy as they were, facing the world each day after breakfasting on a pint of cold ale. But so they did; and at first they were rather scornful of the novelties traders brought home. Sir Walter Raleigh press-agented the Virginia tobacco and potato for all he was worth, but as late as 1631, Charles I was telling Virginia colony to "send back some better fruit than tobacco and smoke." But by then pipes were puffing all over his realm. The first tea, brought west by the Dutch in the middle of the century, could hardly be the vogue at fifty dollars a pound, but it soon got cheap and extremely popular. Coffee arrived at the same time from Arabia via Venice, the London coffeehouses opened, and planting began in the West and East Indies.

England drew on the new world for huge quantities of furs and fish, sugar and rice, and on the East for its familiar spices. The rum and slave trade which was making New England rich did not touch the markets of the mother country directly, for this trade was between the mainland and the West Indies. In general, the commerce of this century was ethically on a par with the pirates of the Barbary coast.

Stourbridge, "the greatest fair in the world," presented the more innocent side of trade under the Stuarts. Italians with their silks, the Flemish with their cloth, the Norwegians with their tar to treat sheep scab in the English flocks, the familiar Lombard and Jewish bankers—these were the foreign guests. And all England came, bumping down the bad roads in a fleet of hackney coaches sent up from London, poling down the Cam and Ouse Rivers that met at the fair ground and gave it the essential waterways.

The fair had started early in the thirteenth century for the benefit of the local lepers' hospital, and was carried on by the town and University of Cambridge with some internal friction; Queen Elizabeth once wrote these joint sponsors to stop their wrangling over which one was in charge of the fair scales. Both the town and university notables took part in the elaborate procession from Cambridge to Stourbridge Field on St. Bartholomew's Day, August 24, to open the fair, and joined in the reading of the royal proclamation that inaugurated every important fair in England. *The*

ENGLISH VARIETY

Cry in Stourbridge Fair bade the crowds "to keep the king's peace and make no fray, outcry, shrieking, or other noise," to lay aside all weapons, and to deal honestly. There followed a long series of regulations about just prices, true weights and measures, and the quality of goods offered for sale, especially food. Since ale was important, there was a special officer called the Lord of the Taps, clad in a crimson coat besprinkled with spiggots and taps, who went from one tavern to the next to sample each barrel of ale. Many people envied him.

In the center of Stourbridge, laid out like a town on a vast field, was the Duddery Square, around which were the shops for cloth and ready-made or second-hand clothes. During the three or four weeks that the fair lasted, a special fair preacher delivered Sunday sermons from an open air pulpit in Duddery Square. The retail street, called Cheapside, was half a mile long, and lined with shops of toymakers, goldsmiths, milliners, pewterers, and the vendors of fairings. Fairings— souvenirs to take home as presents—had originally been relics or images of saints, but now were trinkets of all sorts, ribbons, combs, gewgaws, and gingerbread cut into the shape of hobby-horses and other animals, and then gilded. Fairings of gilt gingerbread were the rage.

Mountains of merchandise from all over the world were piled in the wholesale streets. Half a million dollars' worth of cloth would be sold on the spot in a week, but this was a small amount compared to the indirect trade by orders. The wholesale merchants did business in their notebooks; it was the smaller clothiers who bought the bolts of cloth from the northern mills to take to their shops in Yorkshire and Lancashire. Foreign traders came for the long-stapled wool from Lincolnshire, the best in Europe. Cloth, and hops for making ale and beer, were the big items at Stourbridge, mainly because it was located half way between the wool and hops growers and the factories and breweries.

Stourbridge summed up the whole busy trade life of England, and many people came for its amusements as well. But if they were really interested in the fine points of rope dancing or puppet shows, they would go down to London for the fair being held at this same time, since it was also dedicated to St. Bartholomew; the greatest entertainers of England and the Continent would be there. Bartholomew Fair had once been the center of the cloth trade, and still sold many things besides pears and fairings, but it was first and last an amusement fair. This great popular carnival, which helped to create the theatre, music-hall, and circus, was finally closed in 1855 after seven centuries of fun. It broke away from the old traditions of peace and honesty, it was riddled with pickpockets and rascals, it was unruly and noisy and full of hokum. And it was so exactly what the people wanted that every attempt to suppress it failed.

In England things usually go on very much as they start, and Bartholomew Fair was started by a king's jester. Rahere, "a pleasant witted gentleman" and skillful juggler, was Henry First's favorite clown. Rahere's story is one that could have happened only in the twelfth century: he went on a pilgrimage to Rome, fell mortally ill, vowed to St. Bartholomew to found him a priory if he should recover, did recover, and with his indulgent king's help created a hospital, church, and priory at Smithfield near the Tower of London, and a fair to crown it all. Rahere was now prior, but in his monk's robes he continued to juggle at his fairs, and to build them up by advertising miracles performed by himself or his saint, so that soon the world was coming to Smithfield.

Smithfield, or Smooth Field, had been first the town dump and then a great horse market, and its early career as a fair ground was marked by gorgeous jousts and dreadful burnings of martyrs at the stake. Finally the swampy field was raised and paved, the whole unsavory district, from Pie Corner to Cow Lane, was filled with booths (fair buildings) and taverns, and Smithfield became the seeding-bed for the world's amusements. Smithfield with its sordid, garish past should be the Mecca for the people of the theatre, music-hall, and circus, for it ushered them all into the world. This is not to say that Bartholomew Fair "created" the stage and circus, but it had more to do with building them up than any one thing we could name. Year after year it provided a sophisticated audience to watch the experiments in new amusements, and audiences decide the fate of entertainments.

Until Henry VIII dissolved the monasteries, the Priory of St. Bartholomew drew the fair's revenues, and trading was done inside the Priory gates. Then the fair was sold to Henry's attorney general, Sir John

ENGLISH VARIETY

Rich, and remained in his family until it was abolished. The fair had its troubles; it was closed several times during plagues, and hounded by Puritan police during the Commonwealth. But by 1660 Charles II was on the throne, Mr. Samuel Pepys was building up the British Navy and writing his delightful diary, and Bartholomew Fair reached its peak as a public entertainer. By that time Shakespeare was dead and the English drama created. We can only sketch the development of the English theatre, which was incredibly rapid.

Like the French and German drama, the first English plays were Miracles based on the lives of saints, presented first in the monasteries and churches, then in the open air by strolling players. By the thirteenth century, the English merchant guilds were working out a new sort of drama in the Corpus Christi Day processions held in cities like Chester, Coventry, York, Cambridge, and London. Each guild was responsible for a certain section of the procession, and had big floats with a dressing-room below and an open stage above, and as the pageant moved through the streets it would stop while each guild performed its part of a Bible story. Then it would move on, so that the crowds saw one incident after another, like the acts of a play.

From the first, there was horseplay in the Miracles and in the Mysteries based on Bible stories which were the next step in the drama. In Chester's famous Pageant of the Flood, Noah and his wife quarrel incessantly. But then, the Church was used to horseplay. At the annual Feast of Fools celebrated in the churches, everything was turned upside down, and some little subdeacon exchanged places with the bishop. In Provins an ass was dressed in the bishop's robes and solemnly led to the altar. It was like the Roman Saturnalia, when masters waited on their own slaves.

At any rate, these plays or "disguisings" grew away from the Church and were taken over by companies of strolling players who were often under the patronage of a lord. For instance, there was the Earl of Leicester's Company that trouped the country fairs. As the Miracles and Mysteries staled, the Moralities were invented, in which qualities like Vice and Virtue were personified; Vice was always dressed as a clown. Finally the unknown playwrights who wrote the short scripts drew on history and legend, and began adapting the classic Greek dramas, the stories of Damon and

Pythias, Anthony and Cleopatra, the Siege of Troy, eventually creating purely English plays like *Gammer Gurton's Needle*. All these productions were extremely simple: four actors, a boy for women's parts, and boards on a trestle. They were not much more elaborate when Shakespeare wrote his plays; genius needs few "props." Mozart, living before symphony orchestras, wrote symphonies; and Shakespeare wrote for the bare boards of his day plays so rich in poetry and dramatic invention that they inspired the technical growth of the theatre.

Bartholomew Fair watched every stage of this experiment. The London company of Clerkenwell near Smithfield presented there as their first plays the Miracles of St. Bartholomew, which Rahere had exploited so shrewdly. The Clerkenwell players began acting on a high stage out in Smithfield, with the audience sitting on the rising ground around it. In the early plays the stage was built on three levels to represent Earth, Heaven, and Hell. At one corner of Earth there was a yawning Hell-Mouth through which fiends climbed up to claim their victims. Some of these Hell-Mouths were on hinges and could open and shut, which delighted the audience. The Devil was always a comic character done up in a leather robe trimmed with feathers or fringes of hair. When the Creation was played, hares and flocks of pigeons were let loose among the crowds.

Drama grew up and went out into the great world, and by Pepys' time there were several theatres in London. But the theatre was always coming back to the fair, which kept it alive during the Puritan days when the stage was suppressed. Even then the Red Bull Theatre near the fair was kept open by hook or crook, and the arts of the theatre were constantly being built up in the plays presented in the fair booths.

One of the most popular plays was about the fair itself—Ben Jonson's *Bartholomew Fair,* presented first in 1614, and revived after the Commonwealth. It is a roistering farce in which Adam Overdo, Judge of the Court of Piepowders, walks the fair disguised as a king's fool to see for himself whether it is as wicked as people claim. He finds plenty of knavery, especially in the tent of Dame Ursula, the Roast Pig Woman, which is headquarters for a band of pickpockets. The play is full of the fair cries: Lanthorn Leatherhead, the toyman shouting, "What do you lack? What is't you buy? Rattles, drums, hobby-horses, fiddles, babies?" (Bartholomew Babies were dolls.) Next him Joan Trash, the gilt gingerbread woman pleads, "Will your worship buy any gingerbread, very good bread, comfortable bread?" and her neighbor wheedles, "Buy a mousetrap, a mousetrap, or a tormentor for a flea?"

Bartholomew Fair had its part in building up the English theatre, but its really important work was molding the circus, vaudeville, and fair midway amusements. It gathered up all the random entertainments that had wandered in and out of fairs for centuries, and combined them into new forms. Till the middle of the seventeenth century, the skilled entertainers had trouped the fairs as solo artists—dancers, singers, acrobats, jugglers, magicians, animal trainers, and whatnot —each doing his turn and scrambling for pennies. Bartholomew Fair not only combined these attractions into shows, but it built up the skill of the entertainers to such a high pitch that they were in demand all over Europe. And it brought over from the Continent its best performers, so that the fair was really a forcing ground for perfecting the act or turn of performers, who learned from each other and from the reaction of a highly critical audience how to put their acts across, and to improve them.

Bartholomew Fair, at the time that Mr. Pepys was writing his diary, started "music booths," which had music alternating with the turns of the solo artists. This was one of those simple and inevitable ideas that travel far. Call it vaudeville, variety, cabaret, revue, Follies, Chauve-Souris—this form of amusement is nothing but the combination of turns. The very same artists who appear in music-halls may be seen in the circus ring and sideshow, and in fair midways. The circus, like the music-hall, is built up from units; in the circus, animals are the main attraction, and in the music-hall, singing, dancing, and playing.

By the time the music booths started, Bartholomew Fair was running for two weeks instead of the original three days, so that people could see the new sort of amusement several times. The first music booths had two sure fire features: puppet shows and the rope dancing of Jacob Hall. Everybody adored the marionettes, especially since Punch and Judy had been invented, taking a place in the public affections such as Donald

ENGLISH VARIETY

Duck and Ferdinand now occupy. Other favorites were the sorrows of Griselda, the pranks of Merry Andrew, and the adventures of Dick Whittington. As for Jacob Hall, he was the spellbinder of that heyday of rope dancing. He was so graceful that Dryden wrote a poem about him, and so handsome that the King's friends Lady Castlemaine and "pretty witty Nell Gwynn" were both in love with him.

The Restoration audiences knew the ropes—low, high, slack, and sloping—and performers from abroad competed with the English in creating new feats. Monkeys and hares were taught to dance the ropes. John Evelyn in his diary describes a turn in which monkeys and apes pranced out on the ropes, took off their little hats and saluted the crowds, and turned somersaults holding baskets of eggs and lighted candles. A foreign dancer called "The Turk" performed blindfold on the high rope, "with a boy of twelve years tied to one of his feet about twenty feet beneath him, dangling as he danced, yet he moved as nimbly as if it had been but a feather."

There was no circus yet, but it had very nearly arrived. For some time kings had been collecting menageries, an expensive business then, and Bartholomew exhibited its first menagerie in 1708. Meanwhile in the 1660's there were wonderful animals to be gazed at. One handbill read: "Just arrived from Abroad, and are now to be seen or sold, at the first house on the pavement from the end of Hosier Lane: a large and beautiful young Camel, from Grand Cairo in Egypt. This creature is twenty-five years old; his head and neck are like those of a deer." And then there were circus acts being created, like that of William Stokes and his trained horses. He would run along beside the horses, and leap over one, then over two, and finally jump from the ground to the horse's back. Old stuff? It was new in 1652. The clown, the trained dogs and monkeys and bears, the tumblers, the wrestlers and contortionists—all were perfecting themselves for the day of the canvas tent.

And there was the rest of the motley crew that had wandered over England since long before the Conquest as minstrels and glee-men scratching up a living, as Shakespeare says in *Love's Labour Lost*:

> He is wit's pedler, and retails his wares
> At wakes and wassails, meetings, markets, fairs.

ENGLISH VARIETY

These peddlers of fun, Hocus-Pocus the Magician, the Bearded Lady, the Tattooed Man, the Patent Medicine Man with his clown and Jack-pudding monkey, the giants and dwarfs—the whole circus sideshow was at Bartholomew. There was always a trained horse which could tell the number of pence in any silver coin. People still talked of the bay horse Morocco and his trainer Banks, who had toured Europe and never come back; they said Banks was burned as a magician. Shakespeare saw Morocco; and Mr. Pepys the Dancing Mare which, when told to pick out the greatest flirt in the crowd, picked out Mr. Pepys himself, to his glee. Dwarfs were advertised as changelings—fairy children substituted in the cradle for real babies. Bartholomew had its press-agents. It had also its Master of the Revels, who licensed all entertainers.

In Mr. Pepys' time the old ceremonies opening the fair were revived, against the protests of the professional fair people, who resented a counter attraction. But it was a gorgeous piece of pageantry and part of the fair tradition, and the costumes for everybody in the horseback procession were set down in old rules. The Lord Mayor wore a scarlet gown, a gold chain

THE BOOK OF FAIRS

with the Golden Fleece, and the Order of the Garter. His twelve aldermen in violet gowns, the sheriffs and clerks, and all the city officials followed, and at Smithfield the cavalcade paused while the King's proclamation opening the fair was read in two places. Then they all sat in a pavilion in Smithfield while two by two the best wrestlers in England competed for prizes. After this, a parcel of live rabbits was turned loose, and the small boys chased them all over the field. On the second day there was an archery tournament, and on the third a hunt over Smithfield.

In 1668 Mr. Pepys went to the fair six times, though he was in the midst of pressing matters at the Admiralty. On August 27th, he took his wife and some friends to see the rope dancing; two days later they went back to see the "ridiculous little stage-play called Merry Andrew, a foolish thing, but seen by everybody: and so to Jacob Hall's dancing of the ropes; a thing worth seeing, and mightily followed." On the 31st, Mr. Pepys dined alone at Hercules-Pillars on Fleet Street while he sent his shoe to be mended, went to *Hamlet* at the Duke of York's playhouse, and topped off the evening with Punch and Judy at the fair. The next day he had his amusing encounter with the Dancing Mare, which cost him a shilling tip. On September 4th, with his wife and some friends, he observed the Bartholomew custom of eating roast pork: "To the Fair, and there, at the old house, did eat a pig, and was pretty merry, but saw no sights, my wife having a mind to see *Bartholomew Fair,* with puppets." (There was a puppet show as part of Jonson's play, often omitted to shorten it.) "And it is an excellent play; the more I see it, the more I love the wit of it." And on the last day of the fair, Mr. Pepys took three other men to see the Dancing Mare, but she was not in good performance, "which her master beat her for, and was mightily vexed; and then the dancing of the ropes, and also the little stage-play, which is very ridiculous."

But the Pepys family was not yet done with fairs. The next day Mrs. Pepys decided to go up to Stourbridge Fair, and while she was away, Mr. Pepys had his waterman Bland take him down the Thames to Southwark Fair. This was an old and rather disreputable carnival, but it came along after Bartholomew closed, and so had some of the same attractions. Mr. Pepys left his valuables with his waterman, who waited for him at the

Bear—a famous ring where bears were baited and prize fights held. Here is Mr. Pepys' entry:

"To Southwarke-Fair, very dirty, and there saw the puppet-show of Whittington, which was pretty to see; and how that idle thing do work upon people that see

it, and even myself too! And thence to Jacob Hall's dancing on the ropes, where I saw such action as I never saw before, and mightily worth seeing; and here took acquaintance with a fellow that carried me to a tavern, whither came the music of this booth [the music-hall orchestra] and by and by Jacob Hall himself, with whom I had a great mind to speak, to hear whether he had ever any mischief by falls in his time. He told me, 'Yes, many, but never to the breaking of a limb:' he seems a mighty strong man. So, giving them a bottle or two of wine, I away . . . to the Beare, where

Bland, my waterman, waited for me with gold and other things he kept for me, to the value of £40 and more, which I had about me, for fear of my pockets being cut. So by link-light through the bridge, it being mighty dark, but still weather, and so home."

8

WEST MEETS EAST

EUROPE'S last great medieval fair, Nizhni Novgorod on the middle Volga, survived until 1930, for the simple reason that Russia itself is medieval. In spite of its modern revolution and thin varnish of machine culture, the U.S.S.R. is a vast, sprawling, barbaric country made up of many peoples, some of which have not even arrived at a medieval stage of development, but are as primitive as Bushmen. Russia,

WEST MEETS EAST

except for its European fringe, is Asiatic, and Asia has changed little since the days of Kublai Khan.

Fairs grow up at borders between countries and cultures, and Nizhni Novgorod was the greatest of all border fairs. It stands midway between East and West, between forest and steppe, between the Slav of European Russia and the Tartar of Asiatic Russia. And if you draw a line between North Russia, which has always followed Europe, and the South, which is allied to the Turk, Persian, Arab, and Indian worlds, this line would hit Nizhni Novgorod. It lies on the sandy plains where the Oka and Volga Rivers flow together, and so is connected with a huge network of waterways. In short, it is the tactical spot for international trade, and in this case "international" means not only trade with Europe and China, but with Russia's own people living between them. The most "foreign" visitors at the fair a hundred years ago were among the subjects of Czar Nicholas I, and the fair had enormous political importance because it tied the thirty-odd nations of the Empire together.

In no sense had Russia been tied together during the centuries when it was a playground for the freebooters of trade. The Vikings, during their period of prodigious activity from the ninth to the eleventh centuries, dominated Russia from the Volga westward. They sailed down the rivers from the North, portaged their boats to the southward-flowing rivers, and appeared on the Caspian and Black Seas as raiders and traders; four times they fought Constantinople. Their trading post of Novgorod the Great in the North soon became the easternmost station of the Hansa League, and at its fairs the German traders picked up fish, furs, and wood to carry to Lubeck and Bruges. There was a colony of German merchants at Novgorod, which was the Russian capital ruled by the descendants of the Viking Rurik. Later Peter the Great welcomed the English merchants of the Muscovy Company to his new capital, St. Petersburg.

Meanwhile, Russia was ruled by the Golden Horde of the Chinese khans, and paid tribute to Pekin until 1480. Gradually the Mongols were pushed back behind the Great Wall of China, and by 1700 Russia and China had made peace and the caravans were crossing Siberia with furs to exchange for China tea. They were constantly raided by the border peoples, but still they

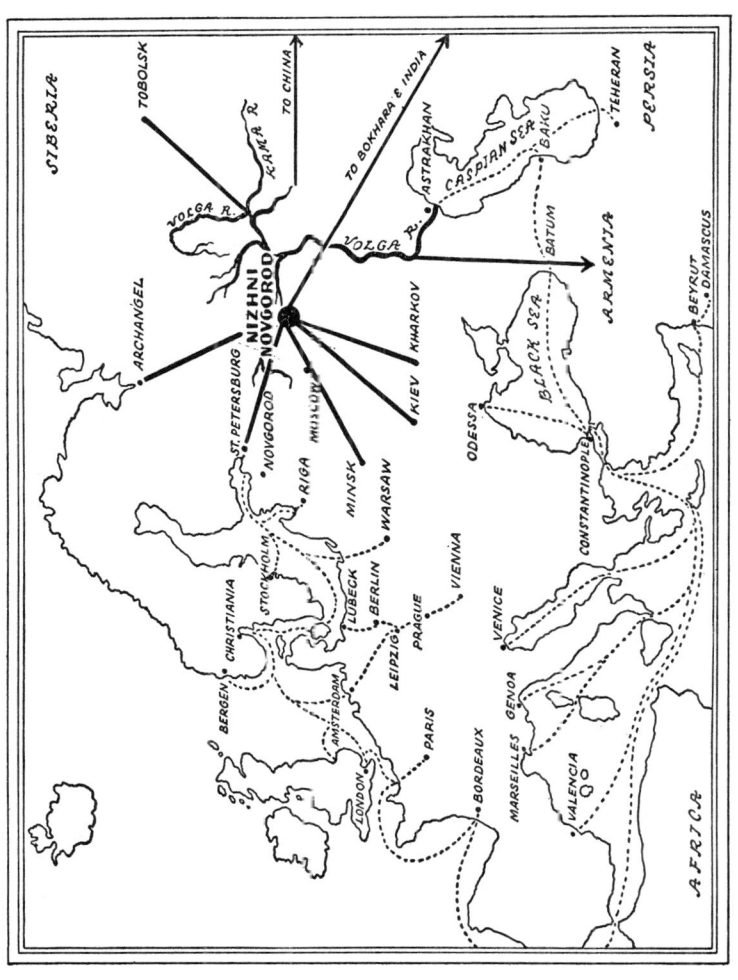

crossed the deserts and steppes to establish the first regular direct trade between Europe and China. Russia, which had been the passive trading ground for privateers of all sorts, now established her own commerce, and its center moved down from Novgorod (New City) to Nizhni Novgorod (Lower New City).

The fair began early in the fourteenth century at the monastery of St. Macarius forty miles from the city. The shrine of this saint had long been a place of pilgrimage, and the fair grew so important that finally the czars decided to collect its revenues, which had gone to the monks. The fair was enlarged and enlarged again, and then was burned to the ground in 1816. This was really a blessing, for the little town of Makaraev was too small to hold the fair that had created it, and besides, it was often flooded by the Volga. So Russia moved her chief market to Nizhni Novgorod, and built a huge town for it on the flats between the Oka and the Volga. The Old Town on the high right bank of the Volga is clustered around its kremlin, or holy city, and from it the great river plain looks like an airplane picture.

Sobered by the fire, the government built the new

fair town of stone and brick, a red and yellow town of forty-eight checkerboard streets, dreadfully neat, startlingly sanitary for Russia of that or any other time. This was only the nucleus of the fair, which spread over an area ten times its size. It had 2,500 shops, each with living quarters above, which merchants could lease from the government, residences for the governor and chief of police, who moved down from the Old Town during the fair, the Grain Exchange, which was the official center of trade, mosques and churches, baths and theatres. On three sides canals made a horseshoe ring; on the open side was the square with the governor's house, where every evening the band played on the balcony, and the crowd walked in the brilliant lights and bought knick-knacks from Persian and Circassian vendors.

The rest of the fair was typically Russian—enormous, untidy, colorful. Every year a second city was built on the river flats—houses of wood, *zinofkas* of matting and bamboo for the tea merchants, taverns and tents and tea houses, an indescribable mélange of goods, costumes, languages, colors, and smells. Until the Soviet Government shut it down, along with nearly 18,000

WEST MEETS EAST

other fairs, Nizhni was largely a barter fair, and entirely a market of direct trade in which no merchant placed orders for goods he could not inspect. That meant that everything sold was brought to the spot; that along the Volga there were mountains of tea chests, pyramids of hides, miles of cotton bales from the South, and out in the Oka a whole island where iron was stored. On another island were the half-wild brave little Tartar horses, who were so used to running in herds that when a horse was sold he had to be dragged with ropes from his comrades of the steppes, who lamented his loss with the most heart-breaking uproar.

The height of the fair was in August, but the town began to wake up in June, as the caravans and sailboats arrived after their long journeys. The Siberians came first with their metals and furs, then the Armenians and Persians who handled most of the southern trade, and last, the Russians and Europeans. The first comers put up their wooden houses and mat huts, and a leisurely retail trade went on until July 15th, when the bishop of the Russian Orthodox Church opened the fair with a solemn mass, and with his clergy went to a banquet tendered by the governor of the province.

By this time the shops in the inner city were open, and the Russian and European merchants were unpacking their cloths, furs, dyed leathers, and manufactured goods, and were inspecting each other's wares and planning their purchases. But buying and selling was held off for the great event of the fair—the arrival of the tea boats that came up the Volga at the finish of a 7,000 mile journey by caravan and river boat from the Chinese tea fields. The trip took from eighteen months to three years of the hardest and most dangerous travel. And yet late in July—the waiting merchants never knew the day—the China tea would arrive, and sales would begin early in August, starting the real fair. "The price of tea decides everything" was the slogan. As tea went, so went the whole price scale of the fair, and the whole course of trade in Nicholas' realm for the next year. Russia's business year began in those first days in August when the price of tea was set.

The caravans which brought Chinese goods to Nizhni Novgorod made one of the great odysseys of trade. The Siberian merchants who composed them planned to arrive at the borders of China for the big Kiatka Fair in

December, where they traded cloth and furs for some 17,000,000 pounds of North China tea, and other Chinese specialties like silk. There was a regular industry at Kiatka for packing tea for its long journey. It was put first in wooden boxes, then covered with bamboo fiber, then a strong bullhide was stretched watertight around each case. The caravans now started back, hoping to reach the Irbit Fair in Siberia within a year; sometimes it took them two. They crossed mountains, deserts, steppes, using camels, donkeys, or horses, depending on the region. Every now and then the freight would be transferred to boats and shipped along a Siberian river. All these changes in the set-up of the caravan meant of course that beasts or boats were waiting at the right times and places, which, barring floods, dust storms, or Asiatic temperaments, they were.

Eventually, using sledges across the snow fields, they would arrive at the Irbit Fair in February, and trade in some of their goods for furs and leather. Then they would come down to the headwaters of the Kama River and wait. If the snows were heavy enough, the traders could by spring float their tea down the Kama, which flowed into the Volga below Nizhni. If the Kama was too dry, the caravans settled down on her banks, raised a crop, and dug in for the winter. This fantastic trip went on until our century, while the English, after the Suez Canal was opened in 1869, got their tea in a month by clipper ship.

But we are talking about Nizhni a century ago, getting its tea by caravan, as parts of Persia and Morocco do still. As for its furs, another heavy item in its trade, these came from Irbit Fair in Siberia, held in February when sledge travel was good. To this market the half-wild trappers and traders brought the ermines and sables which the Ostiaks had hunted along the Ob River, or the Tartars in the wilderness of the Altai Mountains. There were blue and silver fox, martens, weasels, reindeer skins from Vologda and Archangel.

Nizhni was fed by many fairs—Omsk and Ishim in Siberia, Riga and Archangel in the North, Kiev in the West, Baku in the South. She had close relations too with the fairs of Europe, especially with Leipzig, now competing with London as a fur market, but trading heavily at Nizhni on a mutual tax-free basis. Nizhni was doing more than half of Russia's foreign commerce, and more than half the business of all her fairs together. But seven-tenths of all her trade was within the Empire itself. Nizhni sent Austria its red Russia leather, Italy pressed caviar, France Bokhara shawls and embroideries, and kidskin to make into gloves which she bought back the next year.

But the mountains of tea, iron, cotton, and grain piled along the miles of wharves vanished in Russia; the cashmere from Astrakhan, the carpets from Persia, the dried fruit and wine of the Caucasus, the cotton from Tashkent, and the samovars from Toula. From the moment the tea price was known, the city on the river flats hummed with the activities of 200,000 traders. And yet it was a rare thing to see a merchant go to a shop or wharf and buy goods. Traders were seldom in their shops, except for the first samovar at six in the morning. They were in the tea houses, smoking endlessly, drinking endless glasses of tea flavored with lemon, and nibbling a lump of sugar as they drank, for the Russians do not sugar their tea. Hour after hour they sat and talked peacefully, without the least show of doing business. But they were doing very big business indeed. Most of the Russian merchants could hardly read or write, but they had excellent memories for figures, and a genius for leisurely bargaining. Finally the tea drinkers would arrive at an agreement, and seal it with a simple handshake. They would remember the exact terms of the bargain, and carry it out faithfully, because it was made at the fair.

In fact, the Russian merchant was being regenerated at Nizhni. He had always been a despised member of the shallow Russian society, but now was beginning to hold up his head. He was still rather uncouth in his dress —a long black kaftan belted at the waist and hooked up to the chin, baggy trousers stuffed into top-boots, a dingy neckcloth and a peaked cap. Beside the Europeans in their neat cloth suits he seemed outlandish, but beside the Bokharans and Tartars and Afghans and Siberians he looked civilized. These border peoples were responsible for the barter system that was common practice; they bought nothing from samples, and paid as little cash as possible. The credit system of the fair in general was one-sixth cash, and the rest barter or credit. There was still a primitive distrust of money.

But the Nizhni Fair was year after year civilizing Russian commerce, and in all the welter of nationalities was training everybody to keep bargains, which they would not dream of keeping on their own ground. The fair was run by the governor and his special fair staff, with the rakish Don Cossacks riding their horses all over the grounds to keep order. But the merchants had the final word through their general assembly, which met four times during the fair. This assembly, through its fair committee, had such power that it could place an embargo on the goods of a defaulting merchant, even outside the province.

At this period there were difficulties in keeping the conglomeration of undisciplined traders in order, especially after dark. The local police were corrupt, and robberies and murders occurred. The amusements rather ran riot, but certainly they had more color than later on in the century, when English traders complained that tea was the strongest drink, and the music-halls, except for a French cancan dancer or two and some English acrobats, were nothing to boast about. But that was after the fair was reformed.

In its unregenerate days there were a circus, two theatres in which Moscow companies tried out new plays for the coming season, the casino with its cabaret and gambling, and masquerade balls and carnivals. But the real delight of the fair was furnished by the gypsy choirs and the Cossacks, with their wild and moving songs, their dances with the heel and toe and double shuffle, and the music of balalaika and accordion. No country is richer in folk songs than Russia, and no part of Russia has a more romantic tradition than the Volga, home of the Russian Robin Hood, Stenka Razin. There are endless songs and games built around this knightly pirate of the great river. In one, the Cossacks stand in two lines with "Stenka Razin" in the center. He cries out, "I see a sailboat coming down the river!" At that, the Cossacks make the motions of rowing lustily while they sing one of the many Volga boat songs. Then the youngest and liveliest of the crew does the inimitable dance. That is all; it bored most of the English merchants, whose grandchildren would give anything to have seen old-time gypsies and Cossacks.

As in all fairs of the old sort, the fever of buying and selling was followed by a period for settling accounts. Officially, the fair closed on August 25th with ceremonies of thanksgiving in the churches, but actually it ran on until the middle of September. The Siberian merchants took their red calicos and Crimean wools and started back on their long trek to Kiatka, the Armenians and Persians sailed down the Volga, the Muscovites and Europeans sailed north. The shops were boarded up, the wharves stood empty, and the rivers were clear of their forest of sails. The governor climbed back to the Old Town, and the fair city waited for the October snows. Its business was done, and trade from Poland to the Pacific set in its course for another year.

By 1900 the fair had doubled in size, and was doing a business of more than $100,000,000 a year. British observers were reporting to their Board of Trade that the fair had a long and certain future before it. But during the Revolution, civil wars, and famine, the wood-hungry people of the Old Town went down to the deserted fair and carried off all the wood they could find to keep themselves from freezing. That meant tearing down the stout houses of stone and brick to get their wooden window and door frames; and the once tidy fair was a pile of red and yellow debris.

The Soviet Government under Lenin reopened the fair in 1923, but seven years later the Stalin regime abolished all the 18,000 Russian fairs as not fitting in with a trade program strictly controlled by the Krem-

THE BOOK OF FAIRS

lin. But a traveler today in the wastes of eastern Siberia or along the borders of Tibet would probably run into border fairs, or even Mongol funeral games, carried on by peoples to whom Moscow is a foreign name, though they are its subjects. Until Asia becomes like the rest of the world, it will want to trade in the old ways.

And since this is our last look at eastern fairs, we should glance at two which still keep up the traditions of the days when the Phoenicians rode with the caravans. In Hardwar on the upper Ganges in India, a million people meet every year in a pilgrimage fair. The traders of Nepal and the Punjab, of Bokhara and Afghanistan, bring camels and horses, spices and cloth, to sell to pilgrims who still think that trade and religion belong together. And in Mecca, that old station on the incense route to which every Moslem tries to make his pilgrimage before he dies, there is still a fair of huge dimensions. The pilgrims come in six streams from the world of Islam; the Damascus caravan alone has 30,000 camels. Though the crowds worship at the shrine of Mohammed, the habit of thousands of years draws them to the ancient fair site where the temple of Ka'ba stands. In the old days the pilgrims may have worshiped Ishtar, the eastern Venus, in that place, for her dove has been found in ancient ruins. But the early Arabs drew the people of many countries to the Mecca fairs, and set the gods of each country inside the temple. And the Ka'ba where the fair is held is still the neutral ground for the peoples from India to Egypt, who meet there not as Moslems but as neighbors trading together. It must be the oldest pilgrimage fair in the world.

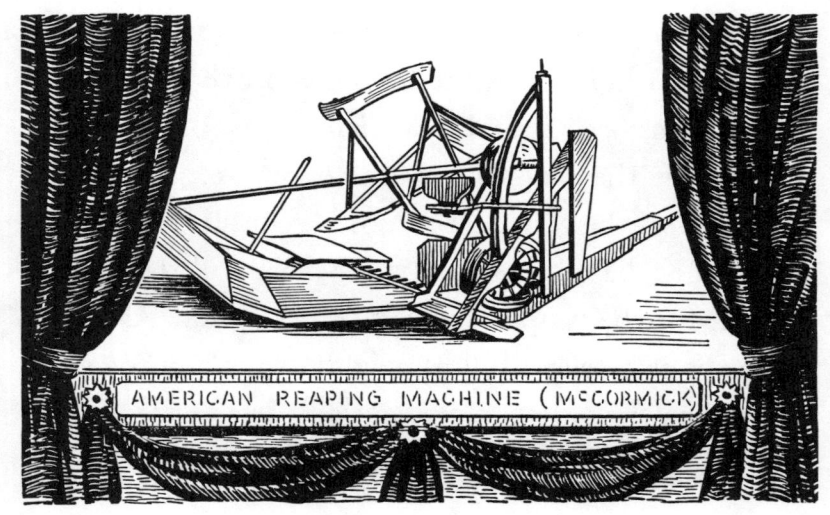

9

THE MACHINE AGE

FAIRS, roughly speaking, have gone through three stages of development. We might call the first ones Fairs of the Gods, because they belonged to a long period when trade was closely tied to magic and religion. Then, beginning with Champagne, come the Fairs of the Cities, in which the various churches played a smaller and smaller part as fairs grew into powerful international markets, each one tied to the city it helped

THE MACHINE AGE

create. The Fairs of the Machine began less than a century ago, when new inventions had so completely transformed trade that fairs either had to change with the times or perish. In this new fair the early religious tie has been replaced by all sorts of social aims, such as international peace and good will, and the enrichment of daily life.

The year the American Revolution began, a revolution of quite a different sort was launched in an English colliery, when James Watt's steam engine was set to work pumping water out of the mine, "in the Presence of a Number of Scientific Gentlemen whose Curiosity was excited to see the first movements of so singular and powerful a Machine." The quotation is from the *Birmingham Gazette*, the first newspaper to be mentioned in these pages. The newspaper was itself becoming a "singular and powerful machine," that had much to do with the transformation of trade, for it spread commercial information of all sorts and developed advertising.

Mr. Watt's steam engine was put to work in the English cotton mills, then in the woolen factories, with momentous results. For goods were standardized for the first time, and there grew up a real factory system and a real capitalism very different from the small beginnings in the days of Maximilian I. And, having started the industrial world on a new path, this same steam engine was adapted to ships and railroads. In 1807, Robert Fulton's *Clermont,* its paddlewheels run by steam, chugged up the Hudson River; twelve years later the steamship *Savannah*—provided also with sails, just in case—paddled across the Atlantic. In another six years the first railroad opened for business in England.

By the middle of the last century, not only were railroads and steamships edging out horses and sailing ships, but the electric telegraph was working, and the first underseas cable was being laid between England and America. For all these thousands of years the highest passenger speed on land had been five miles an hour; soon it was speeded up ten times. The ships that brought the Pilgrims to America took two or three months, but even the early steamships made the voyage in sixteen days. The merchants in Nizhni Novgorod no longer waited for the tea caravans to set the price of goods, for daily telegrams brought the quotations on American cottons and other base commodities.

THE MACHINE AGE

These market telegrams did not change Russia's medieval ways very much, but the machine transformed the western world. The factories were now turning out standard goods which merchants did not have to inspect piece by piece, but could order by swift post or telegraph, or through the jobbers and commission houses which sprang up. Wholesale concerns and retail shops were now firmly established, and so were banks and stock exchanges. Fairs, that had done the banking, stock exchange, and wholesale business of the medieval world, gradually found themselves without a job. Bit by bit they had lost their special nature as asylums and international tribunals for traders, and their monopoly of trade through guilds and hansas and the edicts of king and pope. In the great days of Champagne the sixty French and Flemish weaving towns belonging to the London Hansa were compelled by royal edict to sell their entire output of cloth in the six Champagne fairs. But kings could no longer command merchants and direct the course of trade. The long fight was won; free trade began in Antwerp, and was now the rule. And fairs no longer performed banking and credit operations, for these were taken over by banks, stock exchanges, clearing-houses, and post offices.

What was left for the fair, that now saw its functions spread out into several new institutions? It looked as if the fair had served its purpose, like the horse and sailing ship, and now must leave the crowded stage. The fair is dead. Long live the fair!

Except in the East, the medieval fair burned to the ground, only to grow up from its strong roots and produce a new growth of fairs. Just as the Fairs of the Gods died with the Roman Empire only to spring up into the much greater marts of the medieval cities, so, during the eighteenth and nineteenth centuries, the classic fair died and reappeared in fresh forms.

One new adjustment was made by certain old fairs like Bartholomew, which, as their trading importance waned, specialized in amusements, and survived as popular carnivals. Amsterdam and Rotterdam had their kermesses that went on day and night; Paris her apparently immortal Gingerbread, Ham, and Onion Fairs. But the greatest French amusement fairs which had grown out of big international markets into even bigger public entertainers were St. Germain and St. Laurent in the suburbs of Paris. Bartholomew Fair had done its

THE MACHINE AGE

best work by Mr. Pepys' day, when these French fairs were just starting to experiment with their great contribution to the world—the *opéra-comique,* the play with music.

St. Germain lasted from February third until Palm Sunday, and St. Laurent all of July, August, and September, which gave them long and fruitful seasons. Both had the random amusements popular across the Channel, and both had theatres which were bitterly fought by the dignified national theatre, the *Comédie-Française* (founded in 1680), and by the *Opéra*. For the fair theatres stole the thunder from these young and feeble institutions, stole their actors, singers, dramatists, and librettists, and provided them with a new flexible medium—the play, skit, or operetta garnished with music. By 1678 they were giving operas acted by giant marionettes; then they used real actors and singers to present old Italian comedies in the new form. Soon they created the Harlequins, Scaramouches, and Polichinelles which the ballet later borrowed. And they inspired the ingenuity of dramatists like Le Sage, who alone turned out more than a hundred short pieces and skits. Finally, in a big company merged with the *Opéra*

Italienne, the *Opéra-Comique* played both fairs. It created the modern boulevard theatres, revived the legitimate stage, and as the familiar comic opera was turned to good account by Gilbert and Sullivan and Victor Herbert.

An entirely new sort of fair was created by the agricultural revolution which ran along with the Industrial Revolution. These were the first fairs to specialize in farmers' interests and problems, and they have come to be very important in England and America. We will look at the American county and state fairs in the next chapter.

So there were fairs for farmers and fairs for amusement, led by the pacemakers in London and Paris. The world of industry and trade now created two types—the world's fair or exposition and, late in the century, the sample fair. The exposition was an attempt to get people and goods together again under conditions as exciting as the old fairs. The shops of the last century had not learned the art of display; trade, which had always been a delightful experience for merchants and crowds alike, was getting dangerously dull. The exposition was a product of the new advertising technique that was developing, and which was making trade more and more indirect. In the old fairs, the buyers got their excitement by looking over a great quantity of goods and choosing the particular things that attracted them. Then they bought them and carried them home. The new expositions did not sell goods, but they "sold" customers. They displayed a richer and richer assortment of merchandise in palaces with bands playing and flags and festoons streaming. They created an appetite for new goods, and that is all there is to selling, except for the simple details of handing over money and carrying purchases home.

And then there is that intangible task of the old fairs —the gathering of many people animated by the special good will which goes back to the peace of the fair, the exchange of ideas, information, and purposes. The fair has always educated the crowds. It has informed them of what is going on, taught them discrimination about goods, amusements, and human nature, created new tastes and habits of living, and, above all, given people a sense of living in a larger world than their home town or their home country. The exposition consciously took over this work of education which had been accomplished unconsciously by fairs, which grew out of the needs and instincts of the people, and so served them more deeply. But the exposition has worked hard at this task and succeeded as well as we could expect. For it is itself a product of machine culture trying to instruct and amuse the masses, and the whole process gets rather mechanical.

But the first world's fair, which was in many ways the best of all, was no machine product. The Great Exhibition of London in 1851 came out of the solitary ponderings of Prince Albert, who had felt the tremendous impact of the Machine Age, and felt that it must be given visible expression. It reflected the Prince Consort's interest in industry, science, and the arts, his methodical habits and stubborn persistence. And it expressed Victoria's personality, the force that lay in that gushing, domestic, happy woman who regarded her whole vast empire as part of her adored family, and gave her name to the greatest age in England since Elizabeth's.

As the international fairs had died down, the nations had become stronger in themselves and more and more in rivalry with each other. In order to build up manu-

THE MACHINE AGE

factures and the industrial arts there had been a century of "industrial expositions" in England, Germany, and especially France; all strictly national and conducted in a spirit of unfriendly competition with the arts and industries of all other countries. It was no accident that the idea of getting the nations together in a friendly display of their accomplishments came to a German living in a country which had not yet accepted him except as Victoria's husband. He could not be a jingo, because he belonged to two nations. And so he brought the nations together in the first conscious effort to co-operate in the arts of peace. It was very different from the nations meeting in Champagne; this was an effort, you might say an act of will. As Lytton Strachey describes Albert's ponderings:

Without consulting anyone, he thought out the details of his conception with the minutest care. There had been exhibitions before in the world, but this should surpass them all. It should contain specimens of what every country could produce in raw materials, in machinery and mechanical inventions, in manufactures, and in the applied and plastic arts. It should not be merely useful and ornamental; it should teach a high moral lesson. It should be an international monument to those supreme blessings of civilization—peace, progress, and prosperity.

When Prince Albert had arranged everything in his methodical German head, he called together a small committee and, with its approval, set to work. The colonies and the foreign nations were enthusiastic, the public subscribed funds, but Parliament worked itself into a lather of protest. England would be overrun with foreign rogues who would endanger the public morals, start a revolution or at least a riot, and steal England's trade secrets. By the time this opposition was quieted, there was another rumpus about Albert's plans for the exhibition palace. He had chosen among many competing plans the Crystal Palace design of Sir Joseph Paxton, who had built greenhouses all over the country, and was now eager to expand the idea into a monster conservatory. All the die-hards insisted that the Exhibition should not be in Hyde Park, and not under glass, which would leak and ruin everything under it. Albert nearly wrecked his health in these struggles, but the preposterous Crystal Palace, which taught the world the art of steel and glass construction, towered over Hyde Park like some giant portent of the future.

ALBERT SHOWS VICTORIA THE CRYSTAL PALACE MODEL

THE MACHINE AGE

Though Colonel Sibthorpe, in the Parliament debate, had prayed that hail and lightning might descend from heaven and destroy the accursed thing, it housed the Exhibition nobly, and then was moved to a suburb to enjoy a peaceful old age as an art gallery.

On the first of May, Queen Victoria, almost delirious with pride, opened the Exhibition. The day was brilliant, and so were the opening ceremonies—Albert's address to the Queen, a prayer by the Archbishop of Canterbury, and a huge choir bursting into the "Hallelujah Chorus." The crowds were enormous and perfectly behaved, the flags of the nations floated over the heads of their ambassadors, the arts and inventions of the world were embedded in fresh palms—and the sun shone through Sir Joseph's glass roof. Victoria declared: "The only event it in the slightest degree reminded me of was the Coronation, but this day's festival was a thousand times superior." It was a complete vindication of Albert; as Victoria wrote her uncle, the first of May was "the *greatest* day in our history, the most *beautiful* and *imposing* and *touching* spectacle ever seen, and the triumph of my beloved Albert."

The Prince Consort had done his work well. In the

six months the Exhibition was open, six million people came to see it, and there was not the slightest sign of a revolution or riot, or even indecorum. There were 17,000 exhibitors, nearly half of them from other countries. For the first time the world could check up on what it was producing. Awards were given for the best products, and machines, most of them English, took half of them. But England discovered that she was behind Europe in textiles and the industrial arts, and mended her ways accordingly. The Exhibition gave a great lift to foreign trade and spread new manufacturing ideas around the globe.

The crowds—and often among the crowds Victoria, in a close little bonnet with ribbons tied under her chin, on the arm of her dearest Albert in a white waistcoat and the frock coat named after him—admired the jewel exhibit of the powerful East India Company which displayed the Kohinoor diamond, but stood just as long before McCormick's "Virginia Reaper," and other American exhibits such as false teeth and artificial legs, chewing tobacco, Colt's repeating pistol, Goodyear's rubber goods, and the trotting sulkies used in the county and state fairs. Lothar Bucher, Bismarck's

THE MACHINE AGE

secretary, spent hours watching an English machine turn out furniture, and went home to give pointers to those artisans of Nuremberg and the Rhine cities who still liked to carve an oak chest by hand. To make the triumph of the Exhibition complete, it closed with a surplus of nearly a million dollars, creating a tradition that its successors sometimes failed to follow.

The successors were legion. The world was seized with an epidemic of expositions, some good, many bad. England, which created a perfect world's fair that was a perfect success, never had another that will go down in history. France turned out to have a genius for expositions, and has had the best ones in Europe. This is partly due to the fact that Paris is a matchless stage for the world's fair; it is located in the right spot; it has a river which is both a great waterway for trade and a refreshment to the eye; and it is the most beautifully planned city on earth.

Until the last century, neither cities nor fairs were "planned" in the modern sense. Cities grew up on the checkerboard system, varied by open squares and by winding streets that followed old paths or streams. Since fairs had to have the largest space available, they were held in the cathedral closes, churchyards, and marketplaces, and these were always squares or rectangles. The ancient laws of Chow-li stipulated that markets should be held in squares, with five shops on each side. That merely reflected city-planning habits which are so universal that even now we speak of the green space where the band plays on Saturday nights as "the square."

Nobody seems to have noticed that the square is giving way to the circle, both in cities and in the temporary metropolises which house expositions. But the man who started the whole idea certainly knew what he was about, and so do his successors on modern town-planning and fair-planning boards. But these people make cities and parks and fairs, and talk very little. They create the world we live in, and then suddenly we look around and discover that this world is beginning to be made on the gracious principle of the circle instead of the rigid square, and that probably our lives and thoughts are changing because of this shift, and that certainly we should be grateful for it.

The circle as the basis of city planning arrived in the world at the same moment with the exposition. The

THE MACHINE AGE

first Paris exposition, which came four years after the triumph of the Crystal Palace, was held on the Champs-Elysées in the new city created by Baron Haussmann. Under Napoleon III, a forward-looking man who loved trade and cities, Baron Haussmann took the old medieval Paris and transformed most of it. He ripped out the checkerboard streets and stiff squares. The squares became circles, and the streets became spokes radiating from them, wide tree-lined avenues which created vistas often leading to a fine public building as climax. America's national capital is a muddled copy of the wheel city; Paris remains its inspiration, and, too, the classic source from which the world's fair planners draw courage to experiment with their synthetic cities, in which every detail, down to the last shrub and statue, can be planned as part of one scheme.

Paris has from the first been clever enough to lay out her expositions so that they leave permanent improvements behind. This policy has been possible because the expositions have been in the hands of the government, which has not been niggardly in spending money to beautify Paris and encourage the tourist trade. The Trocadéro and Palace of the Champ-de-Mars remain from the 1878 Exposition, and the Eiffel Tower from the one in 1899. In most countries expositions have been made by special committees which were thinking more of the fair than of the future. It is only in the last decade that Belgium followed France's example, and planned her expositions at Liége and Brussels so that they could be converted later into model suburbs.

Baron Haussmann influenced the fair builders, who in turn spread his ideas through the world and helped improve its cities. But this only begins the list of the exposition's contributions to the applied arts. Here the new fair has found a field of influence never dreamed of by the market fair. Nobody can estimate the influence of the exposition on architecture; sometimes, like the Chicago Columbian Exposition of 1893, it spread a spurious style through a whole country; sometimes, as in the 1930 Stockholm Exposition, which used the modern principles of construction with logic and taste, it set architecture on the right road.

The exposition has ready money and a free field, so the architect can experiment with building styles, sustained by the thought that the buildings that turn out to be horrors will soon be torn down, and the ones that

THE MACHINE AGE

turn out well will rise again somewhere else. For the architect this experimentation is of the utmost value, and has helped make architecture the greatest modern art. Unfortunately, cities and universities have often copied those very horrors they should have shunned, but such blunders are mere details in the general advance of construction. The early exposition first set an example for the grandiose public building, then it began exhibiting in its "streets of the nations" small buildings and houses, and domestic architecture became varied and gracious. Model housing, in which Europe is far ahead of the United States, was stimulated by the second Paris Exposition in 1867, which spread Le Play's humanitarian ideas, and embodied some of them in a very charming model house for workers.

Interior decoration and furniture design have burst all bounds at expositions. The 1925 Paris Exposition concentrated on the decorative arts, and displayed everything from a plate glass house from Soviet Russia to the abstract chairs and ideological tables of the modernists. By 1936, Paris was exhibiting Modern Swedish furniture and decoration styles, and fortunately this return of sanity and domesticity created a vogue that spread rapidly.

As for the pure arts, France always exhibits them as national products. But most of the other countries have the attitude that painting and sculpture belong to some mysterious realm up in the clouds and have nothing to do with the general public. Expositions, notably in the United States, will exhibit machines or architectural styles which are highly experimental, but nervously refuse to exhibit canvases or sculptures which are just as experimental and even more need public examination and criticism. That has only helped to keep art up in the clouds, and kept the artist from having the healthy honest rating the world gives its inventors, scientists, and architects. Some expositions, especially in America, have performed a service by having art exhibitions, often held off the premises, which give fair visitors a chance to see large collections of classic works and sometimes masterpieces borrowed from other countries. But until recently the exposition has missed a great chance to serve the people and the artists who work for the people by exhibiting the current work of native painters and sculptors.

But the exposition, with no such diffidence, has cre-

THE MACHINE AGE

ated certain arts of its own. It should be proud, for instance, of the way it has learned to use water and light, and to combine the two into exquisite spectacles. No big fair could exist without its pools and fountains, but electricity made the fair's night life possible, and also one of its enchanting features—the play of modulated lights on fountains and pools. Modern fairs are best at night, when their fantasy and ephemeral quality are released. Mr. Pepys, stumbling down to his boat on the Thames by the smoking light of the linkman, seems a long way back.

So expositions have fed the human need of wonder and beauty. And they have revealed the new discoveries of scientists and inventors. London in 1862 exhibited the Bessemer process of making steel, and the possibilities of rubber. Germany came to the Paris Exposition of 1867 with the new gas motors and aniline dyes—and the new Krupp gun. Eleven years later it was the United States that created the sensations in Paris with foreshadowings or exhibits of the automobile, mechanical ice box, electric lighting, telephone, and phonograph.

Since the Crystal Palace there have been more than

150 expositions bidding for international attention. Many of them have been conceived in the friendly spirit of Prince Albert, many others in a spirit of rivalry with other cities and countries. Dublin, Vienna, Antwerp, Berlin, Milan, San Diego, Johannesburg, and Sidney—cities without end trying to bring the world to their fairs. Some of them have been complete fizzles, some triumphs, and all of them have in varying degrees promoted industry, introduced the crowds to new goods and ideas, and enriched the towns holding them. As the expositions became bigger and more spectacular, they cost the exhibiting nations large sums in keeping up national prestige. The United States has taken part in more than forty foreign and national exhibitions, with a total advertising bill of $30,000,000.

An attempt to keep this pandemonium of expositions within bounds is now being made by the International Bureau of Expositions which represents twenty-two nations. From its Paris headquarters the Bureau tries to curb the number of expositions, and to have them held one at a time. It does not always succeed.

Meanwhile, the less frenzied world of trade was building up its sample fairs. They are called also trade,

THE MACHINE AGE

industrial, technical, and specialty fairs, but they all present samples of standard goods which merchants can examine and order on the spot; most of them keep out the general public, exclude retail trade, and serve to bring the manufacturer and merchant together. They began late in the last century, and have now become extremely important.

Leipzig, which in the fifteenth century monopolized the book trade to build up her fairs, seized the new field, and by 1894 had launched the greatest international sample fair. She quickly put Paris and Milan out of the running, and by 1937 was attracting a quarter of a million business men to her February and August fairs. The fair is run in two sections—the sample fair proper, which has exhibition halls by the score in the heart of the city, and the technical section which spreads over a huge suburb of its own. In the spring fair of 1937, seventy countries showed samples, and took orders totaling more than $200,000,000. Leipzig exhibits the latest products in glass and ceramics, textiles, toys, furniture, leather goods, and applied arts, and in the Engineering and Building Fair assembles the largest display of machinery and machine tools in the world.

THE BOOK OF FAIRS

Every part of the globe, from Canada with its Great National to the Dutch East Indies, has its own variations of the sample fair; Europe alone has 160 fairs every year for special classes of merchandise, which are open only to wholesale merchants. England's British Industries Exhibition, held simultaneously in London and Birmingham, is strictly national; France's specialty fairs, including the Bordeaux fair which concentrates on French colonial goods, are open to foreign merchants. The United States, with its motor, radio, chemicals, and other specialty fairs, invites the public to many of them.

This is a formidable development which appears to have an expanding future. At the moment, the exposition takes care of the crowds, and the sample fair clears wholesale business. And as both develop, they show signs of recovering some of the old functions of the market fair. The complex and vulnerable commercial system built by the machine sagged badly during and after the World War. Commercial treaties and international trade suffered, and the accumulation of goods became slower and more difficult. In this breakdown the simple flexible fair stepped into the breach and helped mend

THE MACHINE AGE

the ravages the war had made in commercial life. Since the war, fairs have increased in numbers and multiplied their services.

If there should be a new war on the nightmarish dimensions a war of today would take, our trade ways would be forced back on the long road toward the primitive border fair. Some of us may yet see a revival of the market held under a sworn truce. But meanwhile it is comforting to think that the fairs of today are still a powerful force against the calamity of war. The fair, which first taught the nations to trade together in peace, is still trying to make that peace permanent.

10

NATIVE AMERICAN FAIRS

WHEN we cross the Atlantic to the fairs of North America, we find two very different types growing out of the soil—the Indian fairs, and the fairs of the white settlers. They are both truly native, keeping close to the ground and to the people who earn their livings out of the ground. But the Indian fair recalls Kinsai, and the rural festivals of the white colonists have preserved down into our own

NATIVE AMERICAN FAIRS

century certain traditions of Stourbridge and Bartholomew. So on this continent East and West are finally bound together in the great circle of the world, the oriental fair in its Indian blanket meeting the European fair dressed in the blue jeans of the farmer.

The early history of the Indians is a mystery which will not be solved until we know more about ancient China and America. The best opinion is that the Indians are Mongolians who kept coming for a long period from China to Alaska over the land bridge that is now Bering Strait. According to this theory, some of the immigrants became the nomads who roamed the western prairies hunting buffalo and caribou, and others drifted slowly south and became settled peoples growing corn: the Incas of Peru, the Mayas of Yucatan, and last of all the Aztecs who settled in the Valley of Mexico and founded the lovely city destroyed by Hernando Cortez. The Mayas, and possibly other more civilized people than the Aztecs, had lived before them in this valley. Wonderful as it was, the first great Indian fair the conquerors saw belonged to a much lower level of culture than those that had gone before.

THE BOOK OF FAIRS

I

"Of all these wonders that I then beheld, today all is overthrown and lost, nothing left standing."

That, in a sentence, is the history of the Conquest of Mexico, written by a Conquistador who as a young soldier had gone with Cortez to see wonders, and then destroy them. It is Bernal Diaz del Castillo, old now, and blind and deaf, and in spite of his plundering so poor that he has only his true story to leave his grandchildren. He remembers his first sight of the City of Mexico, a city of lagoons and canals, lying among its floating gardens on the shallow waters of Lake Texcoco, with towers and temples blooming in the water. He remembers its vast and perfectly ordered fair in the marketplace before the temple, the platform in the center where clowns and jugglers amused the crowds, and how a little later he helped erect a catapult on that very platform, to blow the plaza to bits. Today all is overthrown and lost.

But for a while Bernal's story runs like Marco Polo's. The young European ventures into an unknown land, and travels through it with growing astonishment, for he finds a luxurious country full of skillful, patient people making pottery, lacquers, dyed stuffs fine as gauze and exquisitely embroidered, trinkets of gold and silver shaped like animals and covered with gems. The people have beautiful houses and temples and gardens, and "are accustomed to delicate living." Moreover, they are gentle and courteous, treating the stranger as an honored guest and making him costly presents. Finally the traveler reaches the palace of the ruler of the land, and sees a wondrous fair.

From then on, the tales of the Venetian and the Spaniard part company. Marco Polo was a merchant adventurer who observed everything and was content to leave it all as it was. Bernal was a Spanish conqueror, and the Spaniards, as Cortez told the first Aztec chieftain he met when he landed in 1519, "are troubled with a disease of the heart for which gold is a specific remedy." This disease requires stronger and stronger doses; at first the Aztecs presented Cortez with fortunes in gold, but by the time he reached the Great Montezuma, he wanted all the gold and silver in the land.

Montezuma, whom the Spaniards naively called

"emperor" because of his sumptuous style of living, was really elected at the head of an extremely democratic order in which women had full equality with men. Politically, the Indians were far ahead of the rest of the world, as they were in their knowledge of medicinal herbs, and in astronomy, which the Mayas had worked out more precisely than any other people.

In their commercial system the Aztecs were startlingly like the Chinese or French of the thirteenth century. Since we cannot yet trace this tribe farther back than the plains of Utah and Nevada, we can make an easy guess that they were recent enough immigrants from China to remember the Rites of Chow-li laid down in the twelfth century B.C. History is rarely so pat; even if we theorize about the Aztecs and other tribes bringing over the Chinese system of trade along with the arts of pottery and lacquers and many other familiar things, we still cannot explain why Mexico was like Champagne. For we saw French medieval trade growing out of the feudalism that followed the collapse of Rome, and English fairs growing out of the Scottish islands and the Druid hills. Until the future historians prove that the human race and all its ways came from some common Garden of Eden (or until they disprove the idea altogether) we can only say that races go through stages, and that at a certain stage there is a commercial system based on the "classic" fair of Champagne or Kinsai.

We do know that the Aztecs had no shops and did their trading at fairs, which were held all over the country on the fifth day that ended the Aztec week, and that these fairs were also religious festivals and had popular amusements. We know that the Aztec merchants occupied a very high place in society; that they traveled fair circuits in large convoys protected by men-at-arms, and protected also by their close connection to the gods honored by the fairs. Since Mexico had no beasts of burden, goods were carried by the Indians, who trotted briskly under loads of fifty or sixty pounds. The fairs were run by the Champagne system; the merchants had their own merchant law and courts which exercised complete authority; and their council of finance, like the Lombards in Champagne, advised monarchs and made them loans. Like the medieval merchants of Europe, the Aztec traders were really ambassadors who reported to the court on the state of affairs they encountered on their circuits. The Aztec rulers received them after their journeys to get the latest news and their shrewd advice, and addressed them as "uncle."

Merchants and manufacturers were organized into guilds, and—here is a Chinese touch—in Mexico the son was supposed to carry on his father's trade, even if he was too rich to work with his own hands. The Indians were also close to the Chinese in their industrial arts, which required immense patience and ingenuity. But the pyramids left in the Valley of Mexico by the Mayas were in many ways superior to those built by the Egyptians, and are purely Indian.

The little army of 400 Spaniards had been Montezuma's guests four days before they saw the city and its fair. They had spent the time exploring the endless wonders of the prince's palace, which was very oriental in its ostentation and luxury, and which Bernal describes with all the superlatives Marco Polo used about the palaces of Kublai Khan. Mexico City was a smaller Pekin; Montezuma dined sumptuously, entertained by his court jester, tumblers, and jugglers; and gave his dinner service and his splendid robes, which he changed

NATIVE AMERICAN FAIRS

four times daily, to his attendants after using them once. The Spaniards visited Montezuma's zoo, his aviary, and his gardens spiced with aromatic trees and cooled with fountains.

Finally, on the fair day, they were conducted to the marketplace. As they went through the streets, they were struck by the beauty and elegance of the Aztecs. They wore fine cottons gaily embroidered, and over them, since it was November, mantles of fur or feather work. The women wore their hair unbound, with fillets of flowers or pearls from the Gulf of Mexico. When they reached the center of the city, they saw the great temple, Mexico's chief place of pilgrimage, towering over the marketplace thronged with people and merchandise. It was three times the size of the Salámanca plaza, which was the largest any of them had seen before. As Bernal says:

"Some of the soldiers among us who had been to many parts of the world, in Constantinople, and all over Italy, said that so large a marketplace and so full of people, and so well regulated and arranged, they had never seen before."

But Marco Polo or Jean le Marchand would have

felt quite at home. They would have recognized the strict divisions of goods, each kind in its own quarter; the three fair guards in their office at one side of the porticoed square; the fair court with complete power to settle cases on the spot; the clerks inspecting goods, collecting duties and stall rents, checking measures, and preventing fraud. Marco Polo would have described for us just how the excellent police system of the city worked, and how the thousand street cleaners managed to keep the whole city spotless by daily scrubbing and even burnishing. There were perhaps fifty thousand Indians buying fresh food and merchandise of every sort, including animals for pets. But the huge plaza paved in broad white stones was so polished that the Spanish horses kept slipping, and so tidy that Bernal says "one could not find any dust or a straw in the whole place."

By now the Spaniards were getting used to the Indian corn, tobacco, chocolate, and the vanilla that flavored it, which they found in the divisions for fresh and cooked food. But though they had seen many Indian products in the small fairs they encountered on the way up from Vera Cruz, they had not found

NATIVE AMERICAN FAIRS

before the whole richness of the country brought into one place. This was the fair of fairs, drawing products from the many tribes scattered over the country. The masses of flowers came from the floating gardens of Xochimilco near by. From more distant places came the knives and implements of hard obsidian stone, the fine-woven stuffs of cotton, rabbit hair, and maguey fiber, dyed with the Indian cochineal which became the Tyrian purple of the new world; and the matchless feather work. Mexico was full of flowers and of brilliant birds, and the feather workers took the gorgeous plumage of wild parrots and humming birds and pasted them on thin webs of cotton to make garments and ornaments for the temples.

Most of the trade was in the form of barter; for money the Indians used grains of cacao, T-shaped pieces of tin, or transparent goose quills filled with pure gold. Though the Indians had worked out wonderful systems of arithmetic and astronomy, they seem to have had no weights or scales. They judged the value of the gold quills by their length and thickness.

Finally the Spaniards climbed the steps to the temple, where they met Montezuma. With a mixture of

THE BOOK OF FAIRS

horror and cupidity they looked at the richness of the great temple, and its evidences of human sacrifice. Fresh from their own Inquisition and its tortures, they advertised to the world the iniquities of the Aztecs. Cortez just happened to arrive in Mexico when the country was divided against the Aztecs, and the Aztecs, perhaps because they felt so insecure, were having an orgy of human sacrifice to beseech the help of the gods. He shrewdly used both of these situations; the divided country brought him into power, and the hideous rites of the Aztecs diverted attention from his own cruelty. But nothing ever excuses cruelty. Ritual human sacrifice belongs to all races at an early stage, and until now the Indians had never been guilty of wholesale slaughter. But white people, because of the Spanish propaganda, still think that all Indians were like the Aztecs in that black moment of their panic at being new rulers among older tribes.

Before he left the temple, Cortez, turned missionary, asked Montezuma for permission to put the Christian cross on top of the heathen temple. The prince refused with horror, but in the end the Conquest accomplished Cortez's prophetic wish. The people accepted Chris-

NATIVE AMERICAN FAIRS

tianity, but only as part of their old worship; and in their fairs, which still belong to the old and the new gods, very old memories are mixed with newer ideas. Only the tact and supreme sense of style of the Indian could combine all these incongruous elements into one pattern. But in a remote part of the Tarascan country it is still possible to see a first fruits sacrifice that recalls Tailte Fair in Ireland; and, mixed with this deep layer of magic, elements that have come into festival fairs for the last four thousand years.

In Mexico all native fiestas are fairs, and the Indian, who does not change his ways, still dislikes shops, and does all his important trading in markets and fairs. He likes to trade in the open air among crowds of people; his fiestas are the only glorious occasions in his life, which otherwise is poor and without comforts. The Mexican fairs are innumerable and delightful, and every one is different from every other. The best fairs are kept secret from the white people, and are advertised by drum signals or fire signals from one mountain top to the next. The Indians travel for many days to obey the summons, bringing the best of whatever they have to sell, and wearing their best clothes.

THE BOOK OF FAIRS

The fairs of the American Indians of the Southwest would also be kept secret from the white people, if it were possible. These tribes—the Navajos, Pueblos, Hopis, and Zunis of Arizona and New Mexico—have managed to preserve enough of their arts and dance ceremonials to be extremely exciting to the white people of the tourist hotels and dude ranches, even more exciting than rodeos. So Americans in droves invade the sacred rain dances held during the growing season, and late in August throng Gallup, New Mexico, where the four tribes forget their feuds and join in a harvest festival fair. Each tribe has developed its own specialty—the Navajos their rugs and heavy silver-and-turquoise jewelry; the Pueblos their pottery; the Hopis their embroidered homespun linens; and the Zunis, trinkets lighter and more intricate than the Navajo. A most tremendous trade goes on between the tribes at this yearly exchange, for which the Indians save their choicest products. They are more gorgeously dressed than most tribes of Mexican Indians, and wear more rings, bracelets, and strings of coral, turquoise, and wampum. Along with the fair go the Ceremonials, the ritual dances of each tribe.

NATIVE AMERICAN FAIRS

Watching the Indian repeat his pure and ancient rites only makes him seem more remote from the white man, who has never been able to understand him, and so has all but exterminated the tribes of the United States. The Indians endure it all with patience and dignity. The elders of the tribes, who sit in the round clay kivas to direct the affairs of the people, are said to know where the Indians came from, long ago. Where they are going is the concern of the gods, dying like their people. But the bare brown feet of the rain dancers have stamped into the soil of America, so long theirs, the indelible mark of a people we now wish we had understood.

II

When the colonists came to New England a century after Cortez, they left Stourbridge and Bartholomew in their greatest glory. As soon as the new world got secure and settled enough, all the colonies but Connecticut, which frowned on fun, started market fairs on the familiar pattern, complete with piepowder courts. Meetings of a whole community were hard to manage often, so at the fairs there was a lively exchange of goods and livestock and also of tracts of land; people paid their debts and made new ones; young bachelors found wives to take home to the backwoods; and everybody had a good time. Strolling fiddlers and jugglers either came over on the ships or emerged from the forest primeval; for there they were at the fairs, reminding the colonists not so much of Bartholomew as of the simple country fairs back in England. And soon the cockfights and baiting of bears and bulls gave way to the simpler amusements of frontier life—foot races, cudgeling bouts, whistling and grinning contests, and catching the greased pig.

These colonial fairs died out with colonial America. When the Revolution was over, the new United States began to look at herself as a nation, free now of British taxes, but also bereft of British goods. Patriots wore American nankeens and homespuns and in their secret hearts longed for the soft English wool. And the problem of sheep raising was only part of the new nation's farming troubles. George Washington and Thomas Jefferson, the country squires, gave serious thought to these problems, and so did John Adams and Benjamin Franklin. Somehow, agriculture must be improved.

NATIVE AMERICAN FAIRS

Over in England the same problems worried the country squires. Britain was growing in size and prosperity and needed more food and clothing. The farming class just began to emerge and find itself in the eighteenth century, as the merchant class had developed in the thirteenth. Changes in England's land system had finally made it possible for the man on the land to be a farmer instead of a relic of feudalism; the Americans discovered this when they hacked homes and fields out of the wilderness. But on neither side of the Atlantic had stock breeders and farmers gotten together to consider their problems. And meanwhile science had developed to the point where it seemed just dimly possible that agriculture might be taken out of the tight grasp of natural forces, and be improved by study and experiment. With this idea, certain English country gentlemen began holding "sheepshearings" before the Revolutionary War, calling in the whole countryside, scientifically minded observers, and visitors from the American colonies. The sheepshearing contests that gave these early seminars their name were of course part of the program, but every sort of farming problem was discussed, new methods were demonstrated, and prizes offered for the best produce and stock raised in the neighborhood, and also for new inventions and ideas. Out of these manorial sheepshearings the first agricultural societies and rural fairs grew up; and farm production increased and improved in a dramatic fashion.

This whole movement was repeated in America after the Revolution. The most popular rural festivals in America were the Arlington Sheepshearings held on the estate of George Washington Custis, the President's adopted son. Then agricultural societies, very dignified and learned, were organized, with Washington, Jefferson, Franklin, and Timothy Pickering as charter members of the first one, formed in Philadelphia in 1785. These societies offered premiums for experiments and discoveries, and tried to reach down to the farmers by holding exhibitions in which they could compete.

By 1809, in order to make them really popular, these exhibitions were combined with market fairs in some states; but they were snuffed out in the War of 1812. Meanwhile, a charming, energetic gentleman named Elkanah Watson, who had traveled a good deal abroad and seen the English cloth fairs and sheepshear-

NATIVE AMERICAN FAIRS

ings, bought an estate near Pittsfield, Massachusetts, and succumbed to the Merino craze. This epidemic was more lucid than the tulip craze which at another period seized Europe, for it was started in the first attempt to introduce fine blooded stocks to wool-hungry America. But when we hear of $5,000 being paid for one Merino ram, and think what a fortune that was, we realize that the notion of long silky wool had turned the heads of the sheep raisers.

Mr. Watson was a level-headed man, and "practical" was his favorite word, but he exhibited his first pair of Merino sheep with a pride bordering on frenzy, and in the same spirit the people flocked to look at them. They were a greater wonder than the beautiful young camel of Bartholomew Fair, for America knew very little about pure-bred stocks. However, that crazy enthusiasm finally launched the American agricultural fair, after all its false starts.

The kindly and indefatigable Mr. Watson organized the Berkshire Agricultural Society, the first of the "practical societies" which spread quickly and really took hold of the farmers. Mr. Watson's first fair in 1810 was called the Berkshire Cattle Show, but it offered prizes for everything, including jellies and quilts made by housewives. They sent their proudest works of domestic art, but shyly stayed home with the front blinds drawn. There was Mr. Watson in his best ruffled shirt, his winsome face flushed with pride (he looked like a blended Mr. Pickwick and John Adams, if that is possible), all ready to present prizes to the ladies—and they were not at hand. The resourceful man sent for his wife, who had stayed discreetly at home, too; meanwhile notifying the prize winners that Mrs. Watson was waiting to receive them. They came; they discovered it was possible for ladies to come to fairs, to compete in them, and win handsome prizes. Before this, women had been stall keepers or onlookers at the fair, but never part and parcel of it. The occasion was momentous.

Soon rural America was dotted with the fairs of the Practical Societies. And they lived up to their name by serving the real needs of the farmer and tackling his problems. In this period of gentility, there were edifying features—opening prayers by the local minister, choral odes sung by the church choir, an annual address by some prominent citizen, parades, plowing

NATIVE AMERICAN FAIRS

matches—all culminating in a grand agricultural ball. These fairs absorbed the truly American traditions that went along with corn huskings, barn raisings, and quilting bees. And though the country proceeded to get very big and rich the county and state fairs that followed have never quite lost the simple friendliness of frontier days.

Beginning in the 1830's the frontier was pushed far to the west, the McCormick reaper was followed by John Deere's steel plow, and by threshing machines, corn planters, and cultivators. America was trading with England now, sending her shiploads of cotton made possible by the new cotton gin, and grain that was now duty free. The prices of farm products went rocketing, and the farmers welcomed the new machines, for the Gold Rush drained the farms of their young hands. This was a fabulous age for the American farmer. As counties and states were organized, they replaced the Practical Societies as sponsors of the agricultural fairs. The first state fairs were held in Syracuse, New York, and New Brunswick, New Jersey, in September, 1841, and by 1868 there were 1,367 state, county, and district fairs every year. Except in the

South, where the early fall is hot, the farmers' fairs are usually held in the autumn when the farmer has made his crop and wants to take a breath before the fall plowing.

Nobody can possibly estimate the importance of these fairs in speeding up the development of scientific farming. The fairs are the farmers' universities, teaching them the secrets of raising cattle, sheep, pigs, and poultry; of improving their crops of vegetables, grain, and forage. The competition for prizes, one of the mainstays of agricultural fairs, has never lost its appeal. It has stimulated farmers and their wives all year long, and given them something to work for. And agricultural colleges and various government bureaus have found that the best way to spread new ideas and improved methods is through the fairs. The farmers have taught each other, too; throwing off their shyness and feeling themselves part of the whole farming class with its common problems of insect pests, animal diseases, sour soil, and all the rest. As for trade, it has taken the form of tempting displays that sell so many goods. The manufacturers' exhibits of farm machinery and of everything else that goes with country life have a big part in the fairs.

Until the automobile became practical and cheap, the farmer had a lonely life. All year long the farm family had little contact with its neighbors beyond the church and school and the social gatherings connected with them. There was no radio, no telephone. Every escape from monotony depended on the state of the roads, which was often bad, and on horses, usually needed for farm work. So the fairs were the only real excitement of the year. Whole families climbed into surreys and farm wagons and went to the county or state fair, camping near by for a few days. In those few days they stored up experiences that lasted them all year long. The farmer could get pointers on cutworm from a lecturing professor; his wife could exchange cake recipes with other prize winners in "Floral Hall"; and the children, of course, could rush to the merry-go-round and ride on zebras and violent yellow lions.

But the whole family would see the horse races, which have always been the main feature of the rural fairs. As Josh Billings put it, "There was two yoke of oxen on the grounds, besides several yokes of sheep and a pile of carrots, and some worsted work, but they didn't seem to attract any sympathy. The people hanker for pure agricultural hoss-trots." And the people got them. The hankering for "hoss-trots" was double: the excitement of the race, and the interest of farmers, whose very livelihood depended on horses, in these fine specimens which were improving every year. Just as people nowadays crowd around the latest automobile model, the earlier fair crowds thronged the stables where the trotters and pacers were kept. Usually there was a parade before the race to give everybody a chance to admire the horses.

The fairs of the 1870's were in close relation with the jockey clubs just being organized, and some fairs were taken over by the clubs and became little more than race meetings. The fairs began to stagger their dates so that they could form a circuit for good racers; a whole tradition of sulky and jockey racing grew up against the snarlings of Anthony Comstock and other "reformers." Even motorcycle and automobile races have not quite destroyed the "hoss-trot."

And the Bartholomew tradition that thrived in the rural fairs is still lingering, in spite of the midway attractions—Ferris wheels, roller-coasters, and whatnot

"PURE AGRICULTURAL HOSS-TROTS"

NATIVE AMERICAN FAIRS

that swept the country late in the century. Until then, those familiar fun peddlers who have followed fairs all through this history set up shop in every rural fair; and since these vagrants seem to be immortal, they are still telling fortunes and exhibiting the Bearded Lady and the Tattooed Man at such staunch old festivals as Danbury Fair in Connecticut. But in general fairs have succumbed to the lure of mechanical amusements and of the "spectacle" created by P. T. Barnum, the Chicago world's fair of 1893, and amusement parks like Coney Island. It has cost the fairs more and more to keep up horse races, and they make up this expense by letting out concessions to third rate imitators of the big commercial attractions. All this has cheapened the rural fair, and brought in a new riff-raff element. In its amusements, as in many other things, America has been proceeding on the illusion that the bigger and more mechanical a thing is, the better. So county and state fairs have strained themselves to provide "bigger and better" commercial spectacles.

But there are limits to Machine Age amusements. One is expense; and another is human skill. For all the brass bands and spotlights that play as the trapeze performer makes his final breathless flight through the air, it is his daring and skill that count, not the accessories. The commercial amusement makers should realize that while crowds are dazzled by the super-super spectacle, what really fascinates them is human ‚performance carried to a high point. The Bartholomew crowds watched Jacob Hall; the American crowds watch the trapeze artist, the baseball pitcher, the tennis champion; and they are getting sophisticated enough so that they do not miss the fine points. A man still fascinates us more than a machine. And then, as the great Barnum knew so well, people love to let themselves be fooled. The little sideshow developed this game so perfectly that something like it will always survive. As long as crowds listen to the spieler outside the tent and laugh at his transparent lies, and then pay their dimes—not so much for the attraction inside the tent as for that one delicious moment of anticipation when they pull open the tent flap and let themselves believe they are going to see something marvelous—so long there is hope for the human race.

One machine, the automobile, has changed the course of rural fairs by making it possible for families to get to state fairs and neglect the county ones. Some of these have died from neglect, and others have merged into district fairs, but the majority have held their ground. According to last reports, the state and county fairs were drawing in 40,000,000 visitors a year, and paying out $8,000,000 in prize money.

But the "bigger better" illusion has broken down among the farmers, whose bitter sufferings are not confined to the tragedies of the Dust Bowl. The newest rural fair is also the smallest. These neighborhood fairs, which are too humble to attract much public attention, are the simplest possible gatherings of a community in a school, church, or trading center, for a one day display of local products, and homespun amusements. They are fall festivals which recall the friendly husking bees, and they have done a great deal to help farmers, especially in isolated districts. For instance, more than two hundred of these neighborhood fairs set to work with state aid in North Carolina, and in twenty years made the state one of the best producing regions of the South.

The farmer and his fairs keep close to the ground. If he is too poor to go to the big fairs, or if they are too big now to understand his particular problems, then the farmer makes a fair with his neighbors who do understand. The old principles spread by Elkanah Watson still hold good: learn all you can about farming, and have a good time with your neighbors. If all the big rural fairs vanished, these little neighborhood festivals would still spring out of the ground like trees sown by Johnny Appleseed.

11

GROWTH OF A CONTINENT

NEW YORK CITY in the eighteen-fifties was, in the words of its own *Harper's Weekly*, "a huge, semi-barbarous metropolis, simply not governed at all." But this broadside only proved that New York was getting the pride that belongs to a great city. It was suddenly conscious that its police and politicians were scandalous, and its public manners less refined than those of Boston or Philadelphia or, of course,

London, which was still America's spiritual capital. But New York was a metropolis, more than doubling its population in twenty years, spreading up from the Battery to Twenty-third Street. The hoop skirt was winning its place in candle-lighted drawing rooms, and at Harvard the young gentlemen were playing football in top hats. In the better streets one no longer saw pigs, or children smoking "segars." A certain decorum was settling over the city, which laid out Central Park as a suburban pleasure ground, and accepted the new elevators, postal service, and telegraph as indications of an expanding age.

It was in fact a great era of expansion and prosperity. New York was becoming a world port, trading with the Orient, exporting great quantities of cotton and wheat to England—and all in her own fleet. The romance of the Nantucket whalers now gave way to the poetry of the clipper ships, the loveliest apparitions ever to come over the horizon. The *Witchcraft, Gazelle, Sovereign of the Seas,* and *Flying Cloud* sped around Cape Horn to drop supplies for the gold miners at their raw little settlement in San Francisco, then flew on to Japan and China for tea and silk.

GROWTH OF A CONTINENT

These ships were making America rich, and putting even England to shame. By 1860 America had nearly a third of the entire tonnage of the world. We forget the solid facts about how much wealth the clippers created in the excitement of their races, mutinies, battles with pirates, and other adventures. These ships made real speed. Commander Low of the *N. B. Palmer* could make San Francisco from New York in a hundred-odd days, in spite of doldrums, and the passage from San Francisco to Shanghai in six weeks, and could rescue a dismasted comrade in the midst of a typhoon on the way. Commander Low once beat the *Flying Cloud* herself by ten days, and then forgot his triumph while he put down a mutiny.

It was on triumphs of speed like this that the merchants of New York City grew rich; they loved to beat Mother England at her own game. But the New Yorkers still acknowledged Victoria's England as the last word in social matters. The first American world's fair grew out of New York's fresh-won civic pride, and at the same time it was a slavish imitation of the Royal Family's triumph.

So, two years after the Crystal Palace of London

there was a Crystal Palace in New York. Imitations seldom work, and America's first exposition was a complete fizzle. It was started, while the London Exhibition was still drawing its crowds, by a group of prominent citizens including Horace Greeley. A site in Reservoir Square (where the Public Library now stands) was obtained for a rental of a dollar a year; Sir Joseph Paxton graciously sent over plans for another monster greenhouse, but they were too big for the site. Perhaps Sir Joseph had been deceived about the scale of New York's plans by the rapturous rhetoric of its promoters, matched by a newspaper account of the opening, which declared: "In the poetry of notable events the Crystal Palace may be termed the Iliad of the Nineteenth Century."

This poem turned out to be a funeral dirge, for the opening scheduled for May Day, two years to the minute after the London Exhibition, was postponed until July 14th, and even then most of the exhibits were not ready. Local architects had designed the Crystal Palace, and their roof leaked, deluging visitors and exhibits. Though there were displays from twenty-three foreign nations, and as much of the United States as

NEW YORK HAD A CRYSTAL PALACE TOO

could be made exposition conscious in haste, New York was not impressed, and went to Mr. Barnum's Museum to see the trained fleas. The Exhibition of the Industry of All Nations died with the year.

The next year the promoters tried to get their money back by reopening the Exhibition under the presidency of Mr. Barnum himself. But even the Great Barnum could not animate the crystal corpse, so he comforted the promoters by reminding them that after all the Exhibition had helped the general prosperity of the city.

The New York Exhibition was the last world's fair in America to celebrate something that had happened across the ocean. From then on, the fairs followed America's own history and celebrated her own anniversaries. Meanwhile there was the Civil War, and New York threw herself into the work of holding "Sanitary Fairs," so called because they were benefits for the government's Sanitary Commission which cared for wounded soldiers. Little children gave one such fair; New York turned its Knickerbocker Hall into a festooned palace in which the chief attractions were the new sewing machines and a soda fountain. These small fairs were successful and helped to soothe the city's pride.

As the first centennial of America's independence neared, there was a general move for a fitting celebration. After much bitter wrangling between the eastern cities, Philadelphia, as the place where the Declaration of Independence had been signed and the Liberty Bell rung, was victorious. The Centennial Exposition of 1876 was huge, astonishing, and successful. It had a Crystal Palace, because for a long time both Europe and America were convinced that it was impossible to hold a world's fair without one. But this shibboleth was only one of 167 buildings which housed exhibits from fifty nations. One of these buildings was devoted to the activities of women, for by now, sixty-six years after Mr. Watson had inveigled his blushing prize winners to the Berkshire Cattle Show, women had more than quilts and jams to display, and female diffidence had ended.

No amusement features were needed at the Centennial. The ten million people who came were spellbound by machines. They would stand entranced by the sight of a group of sewing machines standing, prim and domestic, in a roped-off space. But there were wonders of the first order, for in this year Alexander Graham Bell sent his first message over the telephone, and this curious instrument was demonstrated by working models, as were other inventions which had been perfected in the short space of ten years—the continuous web-printing press, the self-binding reaper, the Westinghouse air brake, the refrigerator car, the typewriter, and Edison's duplex telegraph which made it possible to send two messages over a wire at the same time. Edison's phonograph did not play "Mary had a little lamb" until a year after the Centennial, and so was demonstrated in the Paris Exposition of 1878.

America was in a ferment of invention that was transforming the familiar world. The Atlantic and Pacific were already tied together by rail and telegraph, which meant that the whole continent was being filled with cities built almost as rapidly as the Centennial city in Fairmount Park. Now America could carry on her heavy trade with India and China in a very rapid rhythm, for goods no longer had to round dangerous Cape Horn, but came to San Francisco for rail shipment east. Thirty days from China to New

York, when the *Flying Cloud* had taken five or six months—that was the accomplishment of the steamship and the transcontinental railroad.

It happened that the Centennial was held at the very peak of this inventive ferment, with the automobile and airplane already on the horizon. The country came to Philadelphia with its mind full of the old Liberty Bell and Thomas Jefferson, and found itself almost without warning in the midst of the Machine Age. The impact was terrific; nobody had been prepared for such a vast exhibition with its foreign pavilions and its palaces full of wonderful American machines. Nor had the foreign contributors been prepared for such a big exhibition, and the German commissioners came home declaring that their display had been both cheap and bad, and that they must never again underestimate America.

But America had underestimated herself. A hundred years, interrupted by two wars, is a short time in the growth of a country. The Centennial demonstrated, in its spacious grounds and gilt gingerbread buildings, the country's power and inventive genius and busy plans for the future. The effect was overwhelming, and released a great emotion of national pride and confidence. The Civil War had deeply divided the nation; the Centennial helped to unite it again in a drive for material advance.

The period which followed was one of almost incredible verve and speed. America had found herself and discovered the machine at the same moment. More flexible than the old countries of Europe, and by temperament a race of machine makers and machine worshipers, America let her new inventions carry her forward. By 1893, just forty years after New York's dismal fair with one building, and that leaky, America celebrated her triumph of the machine.

Nominally this great national festival celebrated the four hundredth anniversary of Columbus' discovery of America. It was called the World's Columbian Exposition, and was held in the new Chicago that had risen from the ashes of the famous fire. The very fact that Chicago, which not long before had been a little trading post, was now a big city ready to welcome the world, shows the speed at which America had been moving.

The world came to Chicago. As a Frenchman sagely

remarked of its 1933 Century of Progress, "Chicago does not give expositions, it gives fairs." This great city, so superb and hideous at the same time, full of the boundless energy and friendliness of the Middle West, is America's Bartholomew. Here the old carnival spirit comes out in a peoples' festival, and the crowds make the fair. The Columbian was gigantic, disorganized, pretentious in its architecture, carefree in its amusements for a world in which Victoria was still Queen. And it was a perfectly splendid world's fair. It broke all attendance records by attracting nearly 30,000,000 people, and ended with a profit. It was America's fair, so big that it suggested the hugeness of the country, so naive and friendly that it reflected the frontier on which the city had grown; and for all its fancy domes and fountains it possessed a robust and moving beauty of its own.

The setting of the Columbian was fine—a great tract lying along Lake Michigan, whose waters were let into the grounds in canals and lagoons that created quiet spaces and set off the buildings. Unlike the Centennial, the fair was laid out in a unified scheme. Its buildings, done in a pompous style we might call frock coat classic, were rapturously copied all over the country; no exposition has ever influenced a country's architecture as much as Chicago's. One man declared, "The damage wrought by the World's Fair will last for half a century from this date if not longer." But then, he was Louis Sullivan, who had built the Transportation Building, whose clean, honest lines people considered too plain. One of the creators of modern architecture had no place in the Gay Nineties; and the other buildings were a perfect background for the women with their puffed sleeves and hourglass figures and their parasols.

Chicago, as the center of the country's commercial life, made the Columbian a fair rather than an exposition by restoring carnival and trade. The big manufacturers spent a good deal of money on their buildings and displays of goods, and got it back quickly in increased sales; and thereafter they used the big expositions as a regular part of their selling machinery. Many of the new inventions were now displayed by manufacturers. Just as the crowds at Philadelphia would gaze at sewing machines, the crowds at Chicago stood transfixed at the sight of rows and rows of electric bulbs, which one could now buy at stores. There was even a house run—more or less—by electricity. The fair itself used a great quantity of the new bulbs and arc lights, creating effects dazzling to people coming from towns lighted by gas.

The year before the Columbian, Chicago and New York had been united by telephone; Mr. Edison's phonograph could now offer a debate by Mr. Gladstone, a lecture by Robert Ingersoll, or jokes by Chauncey Depew; and many people dreamed of owning a phonograph. There were new machines of all sorts—the linotype, the expansion engine, Pullman trains—but though in this year Henry Ford tested his first automobile, the motor car was not yet ready to face the witticisms of farmers who were to put their trust in horses for some time yet to come. But the machine that many people thought was worth the whole fair was the Ferris wheel.

With the Ferris wheel, the machine entered the amusement world. The Bethlehem Iron Company, which built this behemoth of fun, had not spared its steel. The towers were 137 feet high, and the wheel had thirty-six coaches, each holding sixty passengers.

GROWTH OF A CONTINENT

There was seldom an empty seat in this terrifying contraption. Another novelty was the captive balloon, which for two dollars conveyed customers to the dizzy height of a thousand feet. Carl Hagenbeck's Trained Animals competed with Buffalo Bill's Wild West Show, which had everything from South American gauchos to Russian Cossacks.

But nothing competed with the Midway, that pandemonium of delight. It was a trip through the world, through Capri's Blue Grotto and Vienna's Beautiful Blue Danube, with a stop in a Moorish palace or a Hawaiian theatre. There was Little Egypt, there was a whole Irish village making linen. If you were tired of watching Singhalese and Malayan jugglers and acrobats, you could try the Javanese theatre, where the band and the dancing girls were both borrowed from the Sultan of Jokjakarta. As "Samantha Allen of Jonesville, New York," whose books were considered a high point in female wit, reported, "Some women go in to see the Persian girls dance day after day, so's to come out all horrified up, and their faces bathed in blushes." But Samantha found it more edifying to visit the Women's Building which displayed along with

American exhibits mementos of the sainted Florence Nightingale, and from the aging Queen Victoria some napkins she spun and wove herself, and even some hand-painted pictures.

About two per cent of the visitors went to the series of lectures and congresses held in co-operation with the fair, which discussed matters like medicine, temperance, commerce and finance, and evolution. Others examined the model Workingman's Home. But the Midway Plaisance offered the first artificial ice; skating in the summer was something to remember.

There could be only one result of Chicago's smash hit: faint echoes. History was ransacked for events to commemorate; Presidents Cleveland, McKinley, and Theodore Roosevelt patiently opened one world's fair after another. San Francisco, Portland, Atlanta, Nashville, Buffalo, planned expositions bidding for international attention, and ended by serving their own sections of the country. A series of Southern fairs that had come before the Columbian had done that very thing—helped build up the industries of the South during the difficult period of Reconstruction when the piratical carpetbagger was followed by a flow of

Northern capital into the sugar, rice, and cotton industries. These "cotton expositions" in Louisville, New Orleans, and Atlanta performed a real service in spreading better methods of cultivation and manufacture.

By 1904 the country was ready for another big fair. The Louisiana Purchase Exposition at St. Louis celebrated the centennial of the purchase of the Territory from France. It might have presented a romantic picture of the Mississippi, but it took a later generation to appreciate the showboats, exploits of Jean Lafitte, and the dominant role of this waterway in the trade and history of the country. In 1904 the United States was chiefly conscious that it had won the Spanish-American War, and now had a colony in the Pacific as a result; and a huge Philippine reservation was one of the chief attractions. Japan, popular as "the little guy that's licking Russia," showered the Exposition with cheap cloth, china, and trinkets, and Germany sent over an impressive chemical display.

The international side of the fair had its ironies, but the chief domestic exhibit finally relieved the country's long suspense about the horseless carriage that inventors had been toiling over for a quarter of a century. A hundred automobiles were on display, and one of them had coughed its way from New York City, and stood the journey better than its driver, who was a little tired of hearing "Get a horse" from town wits all across the country. It seemed that the automobile might have a real future. But nobody would venture an opinion about flying machines; the first flight had been made only the year before, and the Wright brothers' glider was in its infancy. Still, wireless was proving itself, for in 1902 a message had been sent through the air from Cornwall, England, to Cape Cod.

St. Louis strewed its fair over an area twice the size of the Columbian, its buildings went the limit in bad taste, and it lost a great deal of money. It remained for San Francisco to demonstrate the new art of fair planning, especially in the use of color on the outside of buildings, and to create a gay and charming atmosphere. The Panama-Pacific International Exposition of 1915 celebrated the opening of the Panama Canal, which galvanized coastwise trade on both oceans, for it cut from six to eight thousand miles from the voyage of freighters. Actually, New York should have celebrated this event, for it was to do far more for her commerce than for that of San Francisco. New York could now ship directly to the Orient, instead of buying goods imported by San Francisco and shipped east by rail.

But this city, with its spectacular scenery, its independent culture, gave a fine, full picture of the period, in spite of the difficulties raised by the World War. The idea of the fair was to create a miniature world in which all the arts and inventions should be displayed, to balance the picture of destruction in Europe. It succeeded in this plan, and for the first time built fair buildings as they should be built, with simple lines, courts for sunshine, and lighting and color used for the right effects.

When Chicago in 1933 celebrated her hundredth anniversary, the art of building had progressed to the use of prefabricated materials, windowless buildings using uniform lighting within, and air conditioning. With these concessions to modernity, the Century of Progress went back to the old helter-skelter days, providing rickshaws drawn by handsome college boys to carry weary visitors through the chaos. The fair had a fine scientific exhibition, a huge collection of the art of all times (off the premises)—and another midway. It may not have been a century of progress, but it was two years of fun. The crowds and the profits were enormous. Chicago had done it again.

12

THE PRIDE OF CITIES

IN spite of the efforts of the International Bureau of Expositions to keep world's fairs spaced out, the United States in 1939 had one on either side of the continent. In the life of a city a moment arrives when it must give a world's fair. A fair, according to the economists, results from an accumulation of goods. A world's fair might be said to result from an accumulation of pride—not the competitive feeling whipped up by chambers of commerce, but the pride of cities, a pure and splendid emotion.

San Francisco had just added to her beauty the two greatest bridges ever spun over water, and the sight of bridges creates the sort of emotion that results in fairs. New York City had simply accumulated pride since the days of the Crystal Palace; she had given America its first exposition, a feeble thing, now she could and would give it the mightiest fair ever held. Only a niggard would deny America two world's fairs in one year. Surely the continent is wide enough to balance in either hand its two sea gates, each, as Ezekiel said of Tyre, a merchant of the people for many isles. The fancier of fairs gets only pleasure from this balance of Atlantic and Pacific, whose ports reflect the traditions of their seas, as the harbors reflect the city towers.

San Francisco does not precisely turn its back on the continent, but it does face the Orient. From the days of the Forty-Niners, who went there to find gold and discovered not only gold but the reckless beauty of

THE PRIDE OF CITIES

the Pacific Coast, this city has been unlike any other. Many cities have personality, but San Francisco has temperament, and this gift comes out in her fairs. When the city was impelled to celebrate the Oakland Bay and Golden Gate bridges, she planned her fair with a nice sense of proportion and color. She would have a Pageant of the Pacific gathering in eleven western states, British Columbia, and the countries of the Pacific Basin, dramatizing herself as the lodestone pulling all these elements together. She planned a fair not too big, to last less than a year. With complete frankness her promoters stated that the Golden Gate International Exposition would advertise the West as America's playground, and pay for the new airport the Bay cities needed.

So Treasure Island was built on the shoals north of Yerba Buena Island at the middle point of the new Bay bridge, with an air terminal and two big hangars to work into the fair exhibits and remain after the crowds departed. As long as the visitors were there they could see the China Clippers, the largest flying boats in the world, swoop down from the western sky and anchor in a cove at the finish of a routine flight.

The crowds could also watch the overhauling of the great ships by the terminal mechanics.

Carrying out the Pacific theme, the fair architects created an ancient walled city, and, within the walls, buildings using long horizontal lines in a series of setbacks. In other words, these buildings have the form of the Mayan pyramid or the modern skyscraper, a form, as the Mexican painter Diego Rivera once remarked, which is the native style of North America, and bound to grow out of its soil. The fair architects, bent on blending elements from the whole Pacific Basin in their buildings and towers, borrowed certain Cambodian treatments and used the elephant motif for decoration, transforming the severe American pyramid into an exotic form which the architects called the "Pacific" style. Stylized elephants of wood and plaster crowned the pyramidal towers that flanked the striking Portals of the Pacific; tall lanterns copied from Siamese ceremonial umbrellas were scattered over the grounds; and an oriental mood of fantasy was achieved. As San Diego's Exposition of 1915 spread a Moorish-Spanish style through the Southwest that was appropriate to the region, the "Pacific" style, in a much simpler ver-

THE PRIDE OF CITIES

sion, will probably be copied in the Northwest whose spectacular scenery calls for massive buildings.

The main exhibits were grouped in six blocks of buildings spaced by broad courts, radiating from a central Court of Honor from which rose the Tower of the Sun. The Court of the Seven Seas, Court of the Moon, the Enchanted Gardens, and other plazas bore out their fanciful names by the color schemes chosen for their flower beds and by different lighting systems. Color from massed flowers, from fluorescent tube lighting, and from the buildings themselves, was used from a careful palette. The windowless plaster buildings were painted in warm ivory or in half-tones of certain restricted colors to avoid a violent effect in sunshine or night light. A new method of applying a mica-like substance called vermiculite to wet stucco and painting the buildings with it made the walls of these inside-out buildings glitter with reflected light.

San Francisco "sold" the travel attractions of the West in its "Vacationland" building sponsored by travel bureaus, transportation lines, and all the tourist interests. The outdoor effects achieved indoors in this exhibit were supplemented by historical displays in the

Hall of Western States. California required eleven buildings to tell the story of her redwood area, mission trails, and all the rest, and in her livestock coliseum held a series of shows in which many nations competed for awards.

The Court of Pacific Nations was the center of foreign exhibits and amusements, and while many countries of Europe had pavilions and contributed their Raphaels and Rembrandts to the art exhibition, the countries of the Orient were predominant. Japan built a medieval castle, and the Dutch East Indies a pavilion with bas-reliefs copied from the ruins of Borobudur. Hawaii, Johore, French Indo-China, the Philippines, New Zealand, and Australia, built up the picture of the western shores of the Pacific, and Central and South America the eastern. Pacific House, standing on an island in the heart of the Pacific Basin lagoon, provided a center for a series of international congresses.

The roaring Barbary Coast, after a long sojourn in Hollywood, came home to San Francisco to amuse the crowds. There was of course a Chinatown, and there were of course rodeos. But whenever one of the China Clippers was due to start its flight across a third of the

THE PRIDE OF CITIES

globe, the crowds deserted everything else to watch her take the air. This was real, this was San Francisco in 1939 bidding bon voyage to a westbound ship as not long before she had sped the *Flying Cloud* on its way, gallant ships both, and beauties, that the city watches out of sight.

Since one of the main points of the New York World's Fair was its size, we should begin with statistics. But before we do, there should be a bow to American history, which supplied for commemoration nothing less than the hundred and fiftieth anniversary of Washington's inaugural in New York. Aside from appropriate ceremonies on April thirtieth, and a colossal statue of the first president in Constitution Mall, New York forgot its past in the fascinations of building the World of Tomorrow. Cost, $150,000,000; area of grounds, two square miles; participants, thirty-three states and two territories, sixty-two foreign nations and the League of Nations; six hundred commercial and non-commercial concerns; transportation facilities for 160,000 visitors an hour. This was New York's retort to her Crystal Palace of 1853.

THE BOOK OF FAIRS

It is not hard to indulge in a reverie about a future world, but building it on Flushing Meadow Park is another matter. Logically, we can't make the buildings of tomorrow until tomorrow arrives. But the builders of the fair did manage to create the illusion of a world just over the horizon by pushing forward all the modern elements and ideas possible—streamlining, futuristic designs, unfamiliar materials. With this they mixed pure fantasy, which composes most of our dream of tomorrow. Some of the commercial exhibitors developed the best fantasies—the Ford building with the "Road of Tomorrow" rising in a series of spirals; the inside-out stainless steel building of the United States Steel Corporation; one structure like a radio tube, another like an airplane; a cosmetics building made like a powder box, another like a gas burner, wreathed in real flames.

The note of mystification was given by the theme center with its trylon and perisphere, the three-sided slender shaft and globe of pure white set in the center of the fair. The perisphere, which seemed to float on bubbling fountains, but rested securely on concealed pillars, housed the central mystery of the fair, the

STREAMLINE AND FANTASY

THE PRIDE OF CITIES

planned world of tomorrow. We will return to this after we see the plan of the fair itself.

By working closely with the city government and its gifted Commissioner of Parks, the fair promoters turned a malodorous city dump into a pleasant area with two lakes, the inevitable lagoons, 10,000 trees, and a carpet of healthy turf and bright flowers. San Francisco's 1939 guests left her an airport to pay for their entertainment; New York City was presented with a fine new park and playground, a marine amphitheatre and a recreation hall.

The fair was laid out to make a beautiful design and also to spare its visitors fatigue. Constitution Mall, the central esplanade, ran from the theme center to the oval Lagoon of Nations, its axis continuing to the Court of Peace dominated by the Federal Building. The Mall, with its sculptures, fountains, and dignified buildings, did not indulge in fantasy. The fan-shaped exhibit area radiated from the theme center, and was divided into zones for community interests, communications, food, production and distribution, and transportation. Each division had a focal exhibit built by the fair to point up the commercial displays. The wheel arrangement was emphasized by the device of making a spectrum of colors radiate from the white theme center, the buildings in each strip of color taking on deeper tones in progression.

Planning in the large sense may prove to be the contribution of the fair, for building the world of tomorrow is a picturesque phrase for town planning, in which the general public is just beginning to be interested. The New York World's Fair gathered some of the modern principles of the planned community into a dramatic picture for millions of visitors; and this was a real service.

Into the globe of the perisphere was fitted the model of a city which engineers had worked out with great pains and great precision. Embodying one of the schemes which the government has used for its "greenbelt" towns, the people of "Democracity" do not live in the metropolis itself, but in satellite towns scattered here and there through the broad circle of woods and farm land ringing the city. Speedways whisk the fortunate people of tomorrow into the central city, which has offices, shops, theatres, and libraries, but no factories. These are gathered into industrial towns hidden like the residence villages in the depths of the green belt. City workers, factory workers, and the women and children who spend most of their time in the villages, all have an equal amount of sun, fresh air, and pleasant vistas of green country. They are free from the nervous pressure of congested urban life, and from traffic dangers and delays.

As the fair crowds saw Democracity, it had the appearance of a real town viewed from the air, for they were high above it on balconies which revolved around the inside of the perisphere. A continuous "show" lasting six minutes began with the city in full daylight, then it darkened and its lights came on, and in the vault above the constellations appeared. The little "show" ended on a transcendental note, for an unseen chorus of many voices chanted, and in the sky appeared a dim pageant of the workers of Democracity.

The town planning theme was elaborated in other parts of the fair; in the exhibits of the National Committee on Housing Education, and in the Town of Tomorrow, devised not as a model community, but as a commercial display of modern construction and equipment. This town exhibited one house of glass, and another of plywood, and the latest systems of plumbing, heating, and lighting.

The New York World's Fair, conscious of its vast size, and of the fact that exhibits are today so rich and numerous that people cannot see even a fraction of them without confusion, stuck to its idea of making dramatic pictures. The focal exhibits brought to life the elements scattered over acres of commercial displays. In the Children's World all sorts of amusements were combined into a trip around the world on a miniature railway, with stops for Mexican burro rides, or a sail on a lake, or a drive in small electric automobiles over an "international" highway. Grown-up amusements with a decided national flavor were held in the various foreign pavilions; those that could not be assigned such settings did their work comfortably in the big amusement zone on the shore of Fountain Lake.

The fair even managed to combine light, color, sound, and water in its nightly displays in the Lagoon of Nations, when from the center of the pool came jets of water, gas flames, fireworks, all synchronized with music. Here the fair's passion for patterns became almost overpowering. But New York's fair made his-

THE PRIDE OF CITIES

tory; for the first time the arts and inventions of a period were combined into a functional scheme.

But in presenting this sum total of civilization at a given moment, the fair revealed a rather terrifying secondary theme—the interdependence of the modern world. The intricate machinery of production and trade that we have built up is also vulnerable. Every stock exchange and every household radio is now a seismograph that registers even slight earthquakes in distant parts of the globe. We stand or fall together as a world now.

It is not the business of a fair to show how we can build the world of tomorrow when the world of today is in peril. New York's fair pictured a pleasant world which we could start building today, not tomorrow, from the materials and skills we already possess. It heaped up the rich productions of the entire globe, the present sum of human accomplishment, with the nations gathered in a harvest festival. But in presenting the arts of peace the fair creates certain emotions in the crowds—wonder, pride, and the feeling that these arts must be preserved. When people have before them not an abstract idea, but a television machine produced by a whole chain of patient workers, something not yet perfect, something that needs more time to work out, they want to protect that machine and its creators, and the sort of world that makes them possible.

We might envy Cnossos, which was never fortified, and had three thousand years in which to build up her arts. The people living in Champagne today may envy the medieval citizens who rejoiced because they lived at the crossroads between Italy and Germany. But those worlds were small, and their peace was fragmentary. The people of Champagne were content to keep peace on the fair ground and the roads leading to it. But probably the idea of keeping peace and order in Europe as a whole never entered the mind of the medieval merchant. Today, having made the world so small and so closely bound together that no nation can live by itself, we have been forced to a great effort to put the whole world under a permanent truce. Mankind has set itself the most colossal task it has undertaken on its long road up from the Stone Age.

But all along that road there have been fairs, creating small, temporary worlds in which people can enjoy the actual experience of being at peace with strangers, trading ideas, goods, and hopes. These fair worlds are in a sense artificial, because they are cut away from the great world outside the limits of their special peace, because they somehow make the world's goods seem more wonderful than they actually are, because they make people more attractive and better behaved than

at home. Everything is brought up to a higher than ordinary pitch, lighted up, made desirable. That is the magic of the peace of the fair, which creates within certain limits of space and time the experience of what a really secure world could be. But it does not create the mere illusion of a world at peace, it accomplishes an actual peace for this place and this time.

The impulse of friendliness and good will that generated fairs did not get weaker when men ceased to fear the punishment of the gods. It has on the contrary been getting more powerful and more disciplined. It has al-

THE BOOK OF FAIRS

ready widened the narrow limits of the fair peace into ideas like free trade and the co-operation of the nations in world's fairs. And at world's fairs the nations actually entertain the hope of some day trading under an eternal truce.

INDEX

Adams, John, 246, 250
Adonis, 33-4
Aegeans, 12-5, 40, 56
Africa, North, 15-6, 22, 25, 32, 72, 78, 84, 144
Albert, Prince, 214-20, 228
Alexander the Great, 39, 71
Alexandria, 71, 77, 78, 90
America, 166, 169, 203, 220, 227-8, 230, 244 *et seq.*
American Revolution, 207, 246-7
Antwerp, 137, 145-8, 209
Aphrodite, 33, 205
Apollo, 51-4, 60, 62
Appleseed, Johnny, 260
Arabia (and Arabs), 12, 16-8, 36, 37, 77, 87-8, 149, 169, 205
Archangel Fair, 198
Armenia (and Armenians), 17, 37, 195, 203
Artemis, 25-6, 46, 53, 60 (*see also* Diana)
Asia Minor, 12, 15-8, 30, 34, 37, 45, 84, 88, 90

Astarte, Astoreth, *see* Aphrodite
Athena, 39, 49
Athens, 39-46, 49-50, 78, 90
Atlantic Ocean, 3, 15, 31, 35, 208, 232, 269, 282
Augustus, Emperor, 72
Avebury, 157-8, 163
Aztecs, 20, 33, 233-242

Babylon, 12, 32
Babylonia (and Babylonians), 12, 16, 18, 29, 33, 39, 158
Bacon, Roger, 108, 150
Baku Fair, 198
Baltic Sea, 16, 114, 128, 140, 142 (*see also* Hansa League)
Bar-sur-Aube, 111-2, 118
Barbary pirates, 166, 170
Barnum, P. T., 257, 258, 267
Bartholomew Fair, 153, 172-185, 210, 233, 245, 246, 249, 254, 258, 272
Bartholomew Fair (play), 178, 185
Bell, Alexander Graham, 269
Berkshire Cattle Show, 249, 268

299

INDEX

Bernal Diaz del Castillo, 234-5, 239, 240
Billings, Josh, 253
Birmingham Fair, 230
Birmingham Gazette, 207
Black Death, 137
Black Sea, 30, 40, 45, 90, 190
Bokhara, 91, 199, 200, 204
Bordeaux Fair, 230
Bourse, see Stock Exchange
Breughel, Peter, 137
Brie, province, 120
British Industries Exhibition, 230
British Isles, see England
Bruges, 123, 137, 141-5, 147, 190
Brussels, 144
Buffalo Bill, 275
Buffalo Exposition, 276
Burgundy, 139
Byblus, 33

Cadiz, 16, 113
Caesar, Julius, 72
Calais, 145
California, 286
Cambrai, 119
Cambridge, 166, 170, 175
Canadian Great National Exhibition, 230

Caravan trade, 12-3, 15-7, 32-3, 196-8, 204
Carman Fair, 159-60
Carthage, 15, 22, 30, 66, 71, 72, 90
Caspian Sea, 190
Cathay, see China
Caucasus, 199
Centennial Exposition, Philadelphia, 1876, 268-71, 273
Ceylon, 15, 17, 34, 78, 86, 87, 94, 155
Chalons, 119
Champagne fairs, 7, 20, 21, 85, 90, 107-135, 137, 139, 141, 145, 147, 206, 209, 215, 236-7, 296
Champagne, Counts of, 111-2, 114-20, 123-4, 131
Charlemagne, 112
Charles I, King, 169
Charles II, King, 175
Chester, 175, 176
Chicago, Century of Progress Fair, 279-80; Columbian Exposition, 224, 271-6
China (and Chinese), 20-2, 36, 77, 82-9, 91-106, 148-9, 189, 190-3, 196-7, 233, 236, 238, 262, 269
China Clippers, 3, 283, 286-7

300

INDEX

Chow-li, Rites of, 20, 102, 222, 236
Church, Roman Catholic, 18, 71, 79-81, 91, 108-10, 114, 122, 131, 138, 146, 147, 163, 176
Civil War, 267, 271
Clerkenwell Players, 177-8
Clipper ships, 262-3
Cnossos, 13-4, 47, 52, 56, 158, 296
Coleridge, Samuel Taylor, 93
Cologne, 125, 137, 151
Cologne, Archbishop of, 113, 131
Columbus, Christopher, 34, 154
Comédie-Française, 211
Commercial law, *see* Fair Law
Comstock, Anthony, 254
Constantine, Emperor, 73
Constantinople, 71, 73, 88, 89, 90, 147, 190, 239
Cordova, 128, 144
Corinth, 50, 71
Cortez, Hernando, 233-5, 242, 245
Cossacks, 201-2, 275
Coster, Junius, 149
Coventry, 175
Crete, 12-4, 46, 52
Croesus, King, 37

Crusades, 84, 89-90, 129
Crystal Palace, London, 214-21, 263, 268; New York, 263-7, 287
Custis, G. W., 248
Cyprus, 33, 34

Dagobert, King, 81
Damascus, 37, 204
Danbury Fair, 257
Dante, 108, 150
Danube River, 113, 150
Delos, 14, 51-4, 60, 78
Delphi, 51, 60
De Marignolli, John, 97
Diana, 60, 62 (*see also* Artemis)
Dionysus, 81
Dnieper River, 89
Dryden, John, 181

Earl of Leicester's Company, 176
East Indies, *see* Indies, East
East India Company, 220
Edison, Thomas, 269, 274
Edward I, King, 113, 131
Egypt (and Egyptians), 12, 13, 16, 17, 19, 33, 34, 36, 45, 58, 72, 75, 146, 204, 238
Elizabeth, Queen, 170, 214
Ely Cathedral, 18
Emain Macha Fair, 159

INDEX

England (and English), 15, 16, 17, 18, 61, 72, 78, 128, 140, 142, 144, 146, 155, 157-187, 198, 207-8, 214-221, 246-7, 263

Ericsson, Leif, 154

Ethiopia, 16

Etruscans, 55, 56, 59

Euphrates River, 12, 17

Euripides, 43, 52

Evelyn, John, 181

Expositions, origin, 212-4; Chicago, 1893 (Columbian), 224, 271-6, Chicago (Century of Progress), 279-80; London, 1851 (Crystal Palace), 214-21, 263, 268; New York, 1853 (Crystal Palace), 263-7; New York World's Fair, 1939, 4, 281-2, 287-95; Paris expositions, 221, 223-7; Philadelphia, 1876 (Centennial), 268-71; San Francisco, 1915 (Panama-Pacific), 278-9, San Francisco, 1939 (Golden Gate), 3, 281-7; St. Louis, 1904 (Louisiana Purchase), 277-8; other cities, 224, 228, 276-7, 284

Expositions, International Bureau of, 228, 281

Ezekiel, 28-30, 36, 38, 39, 282

Fair Amusements, 49, 53, 74-5, 103-4, 132-4, 143, 152-4, 159, 164, 172-187, 201-2, 210-12, 227, 234, 246, 251, 253-8, 274-6, 280, 286, 294

Fair Asylum, 26, 46, 67, 126, 147, 152, 160, 165, 209

Fair, Conduct of the, 48-9, 66-7, 69, 101-2, 120-7, 158-60, 165-6, 170-1, 200-1, 237, 239-40

Fair Financial Systems, 7, 37, 48, 66, 69-70, 113, 126, 130-2, 142, 145-7, 200, 209-10, 241

Fair Law, 7, 67, 111, 122, 124-5, 237

Fair Truce, *see* Peace of the Fair

Feronia, 61, 62

Ferris wheel, 254, 274

Flanders (and Flemish), 112, 113, 120, 123, 126, 139, 141-8, 153, 166, 170

Florence, 113, 125, 137, 140, 144

Flying Cloud, 262-3, 270, 287

Ford, Henry, 274

France (and French), 20, 107-135, 141, 144, 166, 199, 210-2, 215, 221-7, 230

Frankfort Fair, 151

Franklin, Benjamin, 246, 248

302

INDEX

Frazer, Sir James, 19
Free trade, 122-3, 147, 209
Fugger family, 140
Fulton, Robert, 208

Gaul (and Gauls), 31, 58, 68, 72, 78, 80
Gallup Fair, 244
Ganges River, 204
Geneva, 141
Genoa, 85, 90, 144
Germany (and Germans), 58, 78, 80, 112, 144, 148-154, 190, 215, 229, 270
Gobi Desert, 92
Greece (and Greeks), 13-5, 18, 19, 26, 30, 31, 39-54, 57, 60, 66, 72, 75, 76, 88, 158
Greek Games, 14, 19, 21, 44, 47, 49, 50, 159
Guilds, merchant, 100, 111, 124, 133, 143, 175, 209
Gutenberg, Johann, 149-50
Gwynn, Nell, 181
Gypsies, 76, 202

Hall, Jacob, 180-1, 184, 186, 258
Hangchow, 98
Hansa League, 114, 128, 129, 140, 142, 152, 190
Hardwar Fair, 204

Haussmann, Baron, 223-4
Henry I, King, 173
Henry VIII, King, 174
Hermes, 26, 47, 61 (*see also* Mercury)
Herodotus, 22, 25, 36, 43
Hiram, King, 29, 30, 32, 34
Holland, 141, 149, 155, 166
Homer, 14, 40, 52-4
Hopi Indians, 244
Hundred Years' War, 137, 141
Hungary, 88
Huss, John, 138

India, 16, 17, 34, 75-6, 77-8, 86-8, 93, 94, 127, 166, 204, 269
Indies, East, 17, 46, 86, 93, 94, 166, 169, 230, 286
Indies, West, 166, 169
Indo-China, 94, 286
Industrial Revolution, 207-8, 212
Irbit Fair, 197-8
Ireland, 19, 58, 113, 158-61, 166
Isaiah, 38-9
Ishim Fair, 198
Italy (and Italians), 25, 26, 30, 58, 60, 78, 144, 170, 199 (*see also* Lombards, Rome)

INDEX

Japan, 86, 262, 277, 286
Java, 86, 94
Jeanne of Navarre, 123, 139, 143
Jefferson, Thomas, 246, 248, 270
Jenghis Khan, 83, 88, 92
Jerusalem, 15, 18, 29, 32, 59, 73
Jonson, Ben, 178, 185
Jupiter, 59-61, 62, 65

Kama River, 197-8
Kermesses, 137, 146, 210
Kiatka Fair, 196-7
Kiev Fair, 198
Kinsai Fair, 20, 85, 94-106, 232
Kublai Khan, 83, 85, 89, 91-3, 98-9, 189, 238

Lagny Fair, 111-2, 118
Latin Fair, 59-60
Latins, 55-6, 58-9
League of Nations, 287
League of Neighbors, 51-2
Leipzig fairs, 148, 151-4, 198, 229
Le Sage, A. R., 211
Levant, *see* Asia Minor
Libya, 30
Lille, 141, 146

Lombards, 111-4, 117-9, 130-1, 141, 170
London, 73, 172-4, 198, 212, 230, 262
London Hansa, 123, 127, 142, 209
Louisville Exposition, 277
Low, Commander C. P., 263
Lubeck, 137, 190
Lucca, 88, 111, 119, 125, 127, 128
Lyons, 73, 137, 141

Mabug, 17
Magellan, Ferdinand, 84, 155
Manzi, *see* Sung Kingdom
Marie of Burgundy, 139, 144
Marseilles, 30, 31
Maya Indians, 233, 236, 238
Mayence, 149, 151
Maximilian I, Emperor, 139, 144, 152, 208
McCormick reaper, 220, 251
Mecca, 17, 21, 32, 49, 204-5
Medici family, 140, 142
Mediterranean Sea, 11-5, 22, 31, 33, 38, 39, 40, 71, 72, 84, 90, 113, 125
Melkart, 30, 33-4, 35
Merchant Adventurers, 139, 142, 166
Merchant law, *see* Fair Law

INDEX

Merchants of the Staple, 139
Mercury, 26, 61, 62, 70 (*see also* Hermes)
Messines, 141
Mexico, City of, 20, 33, 233-43
Midway amusements, 179, 254, 275-6
Milan, 73, 113, 229
Miletus, 45
Minos, King, 13, 40
Miracle plays, 133, 153, **175-6**
Mississippi River, 277
Mohammed, 84, 204
Mongols, 88-9, 190, 204
Montezuma, 235-6, 238-9, 241-2
Morality plays, 176
Moscow, 201, 204
Moslems, 89, 204-5
Music booths, 179-81
Muscovy Company, 190
Mystery plays, 176

Napoleon III, Emperor, 223
Nashville Exposition, 276
Navajo Indians, 244
Neighborhood fairs, 259-60
Nero, Emperor, 62
Netherlands, 139, 140, 141, 146
New England, 169, 245
New Orleans Exposition, 277
New York City, 261-8, 271, 278, 279, 282, 291
New York World's Fair, *see* Expositions
Nicholas I, Czar, 189, 196
Nightingale, Florence, 276
Nile River, 77
Nineveh, 32
Nizhni Novgorod, 6, 145, 188-203, 208
North Sea, 140
Norway (and Norwegians), 128, 170
Novgorod, 140, 190, 193
Nundinae, 62-6, 68
Nuremberg, 137, 144, 151, 153, 221

Odoric, Friar, 97
Odysseus, 52
Oka River, 189, 195
Olympic Games, *see* **Greek Games**
Opéra-comique, 211-2
Osiris, *see* Adonis

Pacific Ocean, 3, 84, 89, 203, 269, 282-4, 286
Padua, 117
Pamir Plateau, 87, 92
Panama Canal, 278-9

INDEX

Panama-Pacific Exposition, 278-9
Paphos, 33
Paris, 113, 132, 134, 137, 140, 210, 212, 221-5, 227, 228, 229
Parthenon, 39, 49, 50
Pax Romana, 70, 73, 78, 81
Paxton, Sir Joseph, 216-7, 264
Peace of the Fair, 4, 7, 11, 21-7, 47-9, 58, 60, 66, 67, 81, 104-6, 113-7, 121-2, 125-6, 152, 158-62, 164-5, 171, 201, 213, 231, 239-40, 296-8
Pekin, 91, 93-4, 190, 238
Pepys, Samuel, 175, 178, 180, 183-7, 211, 227
Pericles, 39, 43, 44, 49
Persia (and Persians), 17, 36, 40, 47, 84, 87-9, 144, 195, 198, 199, 203
Persian Gulf, 12, 17, 34, 87
Peter the Great, 190
Phidias, 43, 49
Philip the Fair, King, 110, 123, 139, 143
Philadelphia, 248, 261, 273; Exposition, *see* Centennial
Philippine Islands, 277, 286
Phoenicians, 12, 14-7, 21, 22-6, 28-39, 40, 52, 77, 204 (*see also* Syrians)

Pie Powder Courts, 165, 178
Piraeus, 39, 45-6
Plato, 46
Polo, Maffeo, 82-3, 90-2
Polo, Marco, 36, 82-106, 107, 148, 149, 154, 234-5, 238-40
Polo, Nicolo, 82-3, 90-2
Portland Exposition, 276
Portugal, 128, 155
Practical Societies, 249-51
Provins fairs, 111-2, 118-35, 176
Pueblo Indians, 244
Puritans, English, 175, 178

Rahere, 173-4, 177
Raleigh, Sir Walter, 169
Red Sea, 77
Renaissance, 137-8
Rheims, 73, 111, 127, 128
Rhine River, 113, 150-2
Rhone Valley, 31, 113, 118
Riga Fair, 198
Rivera, Diego, 284
Roman Games, 60-2
Rome (and Romans), 26, 31, 55-80, 87, 125, 173, 210
Russia (and Russians), 16, 113, 128, 140, 188-204, 208, 277

St. Bartholomew, 170, 172, 173-4, 177; fair, *see* Bartholomew Fair

INDEX

St. Denis Fair, 81, 123, 132
St. Germain Fair, 210-2
St. Giles Fair, 165-6
St. Jean Church, 120
St. Laurent Fair, 210-2
St. Marie, Cemetery of, 145-6
St. Paul's Cathedral, 18
St. Petersburg, 190
St. Quiriace, 118, 127
St. Remy Fair, 147
Samarkand, 149
Sample fairs, 212, 228-30
San Diego Exposition, 284
San Francisco, 262-3, 269, 276, 278, 282-3, 287, 291; fairs, *see* Expositions
Saône River, 113, 118
Saracens, 84, 89, 129, 133
Saturnalia, 176
Scheldt River, 147
Scotland (and Scots), 21, 59, 158, 161-3
Shakespeare, William, 175, 177, 182, 183
Sheepshearings, 247-8
Siberia (and Siberians), 190, 195, 196-8, 200, 202, 204
Sicily, 17, 40, 46, 66
Sidon, 15, 29, 32, 34, 46, 72
Smithfield, 173-4, 177-8, 184 (*see* Bartholomew Fair)
Socrates, 43, 46, 47

Solomon, King, 29, 32
Southwark Fair, 185-6
Spain (and Spanish), 16, 32, 72, 78, 128, 143, 144, 155; in Mexico, 234-43 (*see also* Tarshish)
Sparta, 47
Stenka Razin, 202
Stock Exchange, 131, 145-6
Stonehenge, 157-8
Stourbridge Fair, 166, 170-2, 185, 233, 245
Strachey, Lytton, 215
Straits of Gibraltar, 15, 16, 31
Suez Canal, 198
Sullivan, Louis, 273
Sumatra, 86, 94
Sumerians, 11-2
Sung Kingdom, 91, 92, 94-106
Syracuse, 40, 45, 57
Syria (and Syrians), 12, 16, 33, 36, 72, 84, 88, 89, 90

Tailte Fair, 19, 159, 161, 243
Tailteann Games, 159
Tan Hill Fair, 163
Tara Fair, 158-9
Tarshish, 16, 28, 30, 32, 38 (*see also* Spain)
Thorout, 147
Thucydides, 22, 25
Tiber River, 55, 56, 59

INDEX

Tibet, 83, 87, 204
Toledo, 78
Toulouse, 107, 113, 117, 119, 121
Troubadours, 109, 117-8, 133
Troyes fairs, 111, 112, 119, 126, 132, 135
Truce of God, 113
Turkestan, 77, 87
Tyre, 15, 28-39, 45-47, 71, 72, 73, 78, 89, 90, 142, 282

Uisneach Fair, 160
U.S.S.R., see Russia
United States, see America

Vasco da Gama, 155
Venice (and Venetians), 82-3, 85, 90, 137, 141, 142, 144, 147-8, 149, 150, 169
Victoria, Queen, 214-20, 263, 272, 276

Vikings, 190
Volga River, 188, 197, 202-3
Vologda Fair, 198

Washington, George, 246, 248, 287
Wassaf the Persian, 98, 100
Watson, Elkanah, 248-50, 260, 268
Watt, James, 207
Wells, H. G., 76
William the Conqueror, 165
Winchester Fair, see St. Giles Fair
World's fairs, see Expositions
World War, 230, 279

York, 73, 175
Ypres, 119, 141
Yucatan, 233

Zeus, 59
Zuni Indians, 244